Salute to Italy Celebrity Cookbook

Published by

J.C. PENNEY COMPANY, INC.

SALUTE TO ITALY CELEBRITY COOKBOOK

Copyright 1984 by J.C. Penney Company, Inc.

All rights reserved.

Library of Congress Catalog Card Number: 84-51636

ISBN 0-9611906-1-2

Salute to Italy Celebrity Cookbook

Concept: Harvey C. McCormick
Editors: Peggy Healy and Iris Ihde Frey
Design: Ong & Associates, Inc.
Food Photographer: Will Rousseau
Food Stylist: Andrea Swenson
Prop Stylist: Linda Johnson
Printing: Lebanon Valley Offset

FOREWORD

Each page in this book is an invitation to step into a celebrity's kitchen, pick up a wooden spoon, and let the stardust fall as it may. If the saying is true and we *are* what we eat, it surely follows that a slice of Sophia Loren's Ricotta Pie will make us more beautiful, a sliver of Dom DeLuise's Pistachio Cake will make us a little funnier, and a taste of Lee Iacocca's Ossobuco will make us more successful.

Most of the recipes in this book have never been published before— truly, some had never been written down. The task of gathering the recipes —including some well-kept family secrets—was never dull and was frequently an adventure. Recipes arrived via telephone or by mail, some typed on business letterhead and some written in longhand on royal-crested stationery. Some were in Italian. Of course, those delivered in person were the most fun.

From soup (an amusing bicolored beet red and pumpkin gold broth) to nuts (a Chestnut Torte from a traditional recipe hundreds of years old), an amazing variety of recipes arrived. Some were simple, some truly gourmet. Those that at first glance appear to be duplicates, in fact maintain a distinctive character via differing methods or ingredients. Should the spinach in the pasta pillows be raw or cooked—indeed, are they called Tortellini or Agnolotti? Is Nona spelled with two n's or three? Some recipes specify old-world techniques, yet others recommend the use of food processor or microwave oven.

What was abundantly evident was the love of pasta. In came the recipes for pasta made from scratch or commercially prepared and in every shape and combined with every imaginable ingredient. And with each pasta recipe came one admonition. Just as Verdi specified that the grand march in Aida be played *allegro maestoso*, a chorus of voices instructed that the pasta be cooked *AL DENTE*: "Hard to the tooth," "Firm but chewy," or "Cook less than the package directs."

All of the recipes have been tested. In the process, the occasional missing ingredient was recovered, and the "taken for granted" unwritten instruction was restored. While the recipes were given a conformity of style so that, for instance, grams were converted to ounces, the ethnic "flavor" of the recipes was left undisturbed.

We have resisted the temptation to describe how simply delicious the dishes are. When a celebrity cook said, "This is my favorite recipe," that was eloquence enough. Then too, Will Rousseau's exquisite photographs, which show *exactly* how good the dishes are, make further comment redundant.

What made the recipes even more delicious was the fact that they were given with great generosity of spirit. The responses came quickly and warmly and with a sense of fun. Preconceptions were confirmed: of an Italian zest for living; of the pleasure of giving pleasure; of the belief that good food, well prepared and well presented, is one of life's great joys. Finally, woven into so many recipes was a sense of family, of tradition, of nostalgia for childhood tastes and smells.

And because so many of the celebrity cooks, to whom we are eternally grateful, attributed their recipes to her, this book is dedicated with love, to the best cook in the world—

MOTHER

Iris Ihde Frey and Peggy Healy

TABLE OF CONTENTS

INTRODUCTION

One of the world's great hosts, he presides over the incomparable Hotel Cipriani in Venice, just across the lagoon from the glorious Piazza San Marco and the Doge's Palace. Dedicated to providing the ultimate in service, he is known for his gift of accurately anticipating the wishes of each guest—a remarkable feat considering that the guest registers marking his career overflow with signatures of heads of state, the rich and the titled, and the famous and the powerful in business and the arts. One contented guest, a celebrated artist, inscribed a collage to Dr. Rusconi: "The naturalness of personal attention gives your Cipriani the grace of eternity, now." Care extends to the food, to be sure. Under Dr. Rusconi's fine Italian hand, the restaurants of the Cipriani have flourished. When he managed another of Italy's great hotels, he conceived the revolutionary idea of putting a pasta restaurant in a grand class hotel. To assure quality and authenticity he sent a scout to scour the kitchens of the countryside for the best pastamakers within a 100 mile radius. Then he toured to taste the efforts of the finalists. "An event," he says, "I had been in training for since boyhood." A true "Renaissance Man," Dr. Rusconi is

Dottore Natale Rusconi

a linguist, a wit, a boatsman and an avid gardener. He resides a brief gondola ride from the Cipriani with his American wife, Connie, and their three children.

A CELEBRATED HOST ON "LA CUCINA"

Like an immense, incredibly baroque tureen, the cupola of La Salute Church in Venice, very appropriately pictured on the cover of this book, seems at the point of opening up to let out the delicious smells and perfumes of all the fantastic dishes put together with flair and nonchalance by a group of elegant Italians.

"Salute to Italy" is indeed a celebrity book. In reading the names of the personalities that have joined in JCPenney's salute to the new Italian look of La Cucina (not the Nouvelle Cuisine, of course), I am filled with a special feeling of friendly admiration for my fellow Italians.

How impressive a group of totally different personalities: all connected with America, all living now, all Italians, all famous, all interested in La Cucina. The variety of their flamboyant characters certainly adds the necessary zest to the purity of their recipes. No fat sauces, no heavy concoctions but, most of all, phantasy and tradition, elegance and simplicity and freshness. Just what they propose is simply (and only) the essence of the Italian cuisine today, obviously personalized and discreetly adapted to their contemporary needs or aspirations or even dreams.

I often think of what makes the Italian cuisine so unique and so much in demand nowadays. I believe, first of all, that it is the richness of products which animate with their brilliant colours every season of the year. Italy is physically a long and narrow country, protruding into the blue and salty Mediterranean, with a variety of soils at times very dry or humid or very fertile or rocky, which makes it possible for the Italians to have a large number of products in the same season and at the same time. The sky is more blue than elsewhere. The winds are perfumed with thousands of essences, and everything which grows here has indeed a different, more subtle taste. But, principally, what makes the Italian cuisine great is its simplicity.

Then there is the fact of so many successive civilizations, continually invigorating the Italian peninsula ever since the fifth millennium before Christ. In fact, the Mediterranean basin saw the birth of what is probably the first civilization (the Egyptian). But so many other cultures followed: the Cretans and the Mycenaens, the Etruscans, the Greeks, the Romans. All this means that highly cultured populations were present in Italy at least 4,000 years before Christ. And, with culture, came also the art of living and, logically, the art of eating and entertaining.

It is widely known that when Caterina De'Medici married Henry II of France in 1533, she brought to his court her way of life and her famous Italian cooks. It is also widely recognized that the eighteenth and nineteenth centuries saw in Europe the predominance of the French cuisine. Highly skilled chefs took the place of the fifteenth and sixteenth century "Gran Trincanti," who were the noblemen in charge of carving meat and fish at the ducal or princely courts of Italy. The era of the "Gros-Bonnet" started. The Italians became totally dependent upon these new masters. Our "cuochi" became known as "chefs" or "Monzu" (a corruption of "Monsieur") to indicate the cook of a private house as opposed to one of a restaurant or hotel. All this lasted until the end of the second World War. Then a new gastronomic renaissance took place in our country. The essence of it was simplicity, and we reintroduced to the public our old original and tasty dishes.

And the Nouvelle Cuisine? Yes, I believe strongly that we started it well before the French. Our *al dente* for vegetables or pasta, for meat or even fish (but the latter I do not approve) preexisted the Chinese inspired Nouvelle Cuisine. Our light sauces came well before. But they were hidden in the deep south or in the windy north or along the coasts, perfumed by wild oregano, thyme and basil, unknown to many, well known to a very happy few. Of course, the regional traditions had not been forgotten. It was simply a matter of reoffering our specialties and freshening up what had been abandoned or simply neglected. Even wines were recreated or reinvented to meet with the renewed interest in gastronomy and oenology.

At home, the Italians also have revived, but personalized, the traditional style of entertaining followed by their ancestors. Though adapted to today's busy world, entertaining in Italy is still a refined art. And the Cucina? Always simple even when served by a staff in incredibly elegant crested family uniforms.

Italy is a wonderful country, with so many contrasts and differences. But at table, all Italians are the same. They do not want a dish which is too complicated. What they say is this: "We stop our culinary preparations half way, as opposed to the other Europeans. They still go on mixing their sauces for quite some time. But we digest better and we 'feel' the texture of everything we eat." This is the Italian philosophy — so evident in the recipes that follow.

Natale Rusconi

GLORIOUS SOUP

The Gold Soup

1 small pumpkin (or large winter squash)

1½ cups bouillon

1 tablespoon butter

½ teaspoon salt

1 teaspoon sugar

1 teaspoon curry powder

Saffron threads, crumbled (optional)

1 cup cream

Peel and cut the pumpkin into pieces (discard seeds and stringy portion) and boil in 1 cup of the bouillon with butter and salt for 20 minutes or until tender. Puree in a blender or processor. If necessary, put through a sieve. Return to pot, add sugar, curry powder, saffron, and cream and cook over low heat for 10 minutes. (Do not let boil.) Thin with additional bouillon, if necessary.

The Red Soup

4 medium-sized beets

2 carrots, peeled and cut into chunks

1 small wedge cabbage

1½ cups bouillon

½ teaspoon salt

¼ teaspoon pepper

½ teaspoon cumin

1 cup cream

Cook the beets in water to cover until tender, about 1 hour. Meanwhile, in a separate pan cook the carrots and cabbage in 1 cup of the bouillon, covered, until tender, about 30 minutes. Slip skins off cooked beets and cut into chunks. Puree with the carrots and cabbage in blender or processor until smooth. Sieve, if necessary. Return to pot, add salt and pepper, cumin and cream and cook over low heat for 10 minutes. (Do not let boil.) To serve, into each bowl, ladle a portion of the Gold Soup. Tilt bowl and ladle a portion of Red Soup alongside the Gold—carefully so that they do not mix. Serves 6.

SENATOR
SUSANNA AGNELLI

A member of the famous Fiat
family, she was Italy's first female
mayor and now serves her country
as the first female Under Secretary of
State for Foreign Affairs. She is also a
journalist, author and mother of six.

"Cooking is a very special art;
it cannot exist without fantasy or
'inventivity.' This recipe is a trace of
what can be an amusing, colorful and
original-tasting soup. You can vary the
colors and tastes by using spinach,
potatoes or sweet green peas. Sometimes I prepare barley in chicken broth
and add this first to the soup bowl."

CHICKEN ALBERGHETTI

4 whole chicken breasts, halved, skinned, boned
2 eggs, beaten
Fresh bread crumbs (amount "by eye")
Butter and olive oil, as needed
16 ounces good marinara sauce
½ cup milk or half and half
8 slices Swiss cheese, paper-thin
8 slices mozzarella cheese, paper-thin
½ cup freshly grated Parmesan cheese
Butter

Dip chicken breast halves in eggs. Roll in bread crumbs to coat all over. Fry chicken in half butter and half olive oil. (Butter burns too easily when used alone.) Dilute marinara sauce with milk (makes a lighter sauce) and cover bottom of baking dish with sauce. Layer chicken on top of sauce. Top with slices of Swiss and mozzarella cheese. Sprinkle Parmesan cheese over all and dot with butter. Cook in 300 degree oven, covered, for 30 minutes. Uncover and cook 10 to 15 minutes more. Can be cooked a day or two ahead and reheated for serving. Serves 6 to 8.

ANNA MARIA ALBERGHETTI

The beautiful face with the beautiful voice was born in Pesaro, Italy, where she began her singing career at the age of six. She made her United States debut at Carnegie Hall and has continued to sing in concert halls across the country. It was her role as Lili in *Carnival* that catapulted her into stardom and won her a Tony for Best Actress in a Musical.

"This dish is always a big hit. I like it because I can cook it ahead of time and keep it refrigerated until it is time to reheat and serve."

11

GNOCCHI

4 pounds potatoes—must be Idaho
2 tablespoons salt
½ cup butter (one stick)
2 eggs, beaten
4 cups flour
Salt, to taste
2 tablespoons salt
Parmesan cheese, grated
Meat sauce

Cook potatoes with jackets on in salted water. Peel and mash while hot. Place butter in center of hot mashed potatoes. When butter has melted (about 15 minutes) mix potatoes thoroughly. Cover with dish towel and allow to cool. Make small well in center of potatoes and pour eggs in and mix well. Gradually add flour and salt, to taste. Knead well to form dough. Separate mixture into four equal parts. Sprinkle each with flour. Roll each portion into a roll the thickness of a sausage. Slice in pieces slightly thicker than ½ inch. Gently roll each piece on flat grater, slightly curling each piece. Pieces should resemble macaroni shells. Cook in 4 quarts boiling salted water (cook about ⅓ of total amount at one time) about 20 to 30 seconds. Gnocchi will rise to top of boiling water when done. Gently scoop out with slotted spoon as they rise to top. Sprinkle Parmesan cheese on top of cooked Gnocchi and top with generous amounts of meat sauce. Serves 8.

MARIO ANDRETTI

Born in Montona, near Trieste, Italy, he fell in love with sportscar racing when his uncle took him as a child to view the *Mille Miglia*, a 1000 mile cross-country road race. Now president of Andretti Racing Enterprises, he is a winner of the Indianapolis 500, a member of the Automobile Hall of Fame and a recipient of ABC's Athlete of the Year Award.

"The closest thing to heaven is eating gnocchi prepared by my mother."

13

EDDIE ARCARO

A legend in horse racing, in his 31 year career he led all other jockeys in stakes winnings and won almost 5,000 races. When he rode Whirlaway in the Kentucky Derby on his way to winning the Triple Crown, he said he felt as if he had been flying. But he has never forgotten his first race when, "I lost my cap and finished the race with the tails of my silks hanging out of my pants."

CHICKEN CACCIATORE

½ cup chopped onion

¼ cup olive oil

1 3½-pound frying chicken cut into 8-10 pieces

½ pound large mushrooms, sliced

1 tablespoon olive oil

1½ tablespoons butter

1 32-ounce can Italian peeled tomatoes, well-drained

8 ounces tomato sauce (canned or homemade)

½ cup dry white wine

1 teaspoon salt

¼ teaspoon pepper

1 bay leaf

1 clove garlic

Pinch of thyme

Pinch of dried basil

Sauté onions in large, heavy skillet in ¼ cup olive oil until translucent. Brown chicken in olive oil/onion mixture. Keep turning until well browned on all sides. While chicken is browning, in another skillet sauté mushrooms in 1 tablespoon oil and the butter, shaking the pan frequently to prevent burning. When chicken is browned, add tomatoes, tomato sauce, white wine, salt, pepper, bay leaf, garlic, thyme, basil and mushrooms. Turn the chicken to coat well with sauce. Bring to a boil, then lower heat and cook (barely bubbling) for 45 minutes, turning pieces occasionally. Turn heat to high for about 5 minutes to eliminate any existing moisture. Discard garlic clove. Serves 4.

THE CELEBRATED ANTIPASTI OF ITALY

Alfredo Viazzi, author of *Alfredo Viazzi's Italian Cooking* and *Cucina e Nostalgia* (Random House), owns three popular restaurants in New York's Greenwich Village: Cafe Domel, Tavola Calda da Alfredo and, especially beloved by the publishing world for its good food and stylish blue and white Mediterranean decor, the Trattoria da Alfredo. Critics praise Alfredo's antipasto selections, particularly his creative treatment of stuffed vegetables. As both a chef and a restaurateur, he says:

"To us Italians antipasto is an allegro overture to luncheons and dinners. Antipasto means stuzzicare l'appetito, *or, to tease the appetite. Therefore, a truly successful antipasto demands a careful selection of delicacies which will not conflict with the food served after. The preparation of a well-balanced antipasto requires as much*

Alfredo Viazzi

creativity and good taste on the part of the chef as the meal that will follow. As a matter of fact, a grand antipasto can be a lunch or dinner in itself, especially when served with a delightful wine and a tasty bread."

Antipasto is the course in which Italy's splendid sausages and cured meats are served. The sausage-makers of Italy have been practicing their craft since their guild was organized in

1376, and as we know, practice makes perfect. Some of their great meat specialties include:

Zampone—boned pig's feet stuffed with sausage flavored with nutmeg, cinnamon, cloves and additional "secret" spices

Mortadella—a bologna-like sausage delicately flavored with fennel

Parma ham—ham with a pale salmon-pink color and velvety textures

Coppa—head cheese

Pancetta—a kind of bacon

Crespone—salami made of beef and pork containing ricelike grains of pork fat

Porcetta—roast pork shoulder enhanced with spices

Pepperoni—as the name implies, spiced heavily with pepper

Sopressata—a dried sausage, coarse and spicy

GIORGIO ARMANI

Born in the quaint town of Piacenza, Giorgio Armani has become an internationally acclaimed fashion designer with an empire stretching around the world. Still, he prefers simple pleasures —enjoying brief holidays at his island villa or relaxing with close friends after a long day.

Tortelli alla Piacentina is a recipe he enjoys making for his guests. "It was my mother who first made this dish for me, and it is a favorite recipe. It's a local dish from my hometown—a rather long procedure, but it is so good that it's well worth the while!"

TORTELLI ALLA PIACENTINA

Filling

1 pound fresh spinach

32 ounces ricotta cheese

2 eggs, lightly beaten

7 ounces Parmesan cheese, grated

Salt, to taste

Cut off the spinach stalks and after having washed the leaves very thoroughly under cold running water, drain them into a colander and squeeze out all the excess water. Chop them very finely and mix in a bowl with the ricotta, eggs, Parmesan and salt until well blended. Leave to rest in a cool place.

Pasta

8½ cups flour

6 eggs

Water

Numerous knobs of butter

Grated Parmesan cheese

Make the pasta with the flour, eggs and enough tepid water to bind together a smooth dough that is neither too dry nor too soft—as otherwise it would be difficult to wind the tortelli into the right shape. Wrap the dough in a tea-cloth so as to prevent its becoming dry. Pass the dough piece by piece through a pasta machine (or do by hand with a rolling pin) to obtain the thickness of fettuccini. Make a strip and cut it up into diamond shapes. Place teaspoonsful of filling mixture on the center of each diamond, then fold up the two opposite sides in order to seal in the filling, forming each tortelli into a "sugared almond" type shape. One by one, transfer them into a floured cloth to prevent their sticking to each other. Place a large deep pan of salted water on to boil. Very carefully lower the Tortelli into the boiling water being sure not to break or damage them. NOTE: When the Tortelli surface to the top don't ever use a fork or spoon but prod them down lightly with a perforated kitchen ladle (or such like) until cooked—for approximately 15 minutes. When cooked, drain them thoroughly in a colander, then slide gently back into a casserole or pan adding numerous knobs of butter and some grated Parmesan cheese. Mix and stir together slowly to coat the Tortelli evenly with the butter and cheese. (To obtain a good result, hold the pan by the handles and turn in a circular fashion back and forth so the Tortelli get well-dipped by the sauce.) SERVE IMMEDIATELY!!! Makes about 100.

BRODETTO

4 pounds baby lamb (cut into chunks)

1 large onion, chopped

6 plum tomatoes, chopped

2 tablespoons chopped Italian parsley

2 large, fresh basil leaves, chopped or 1 teaspoon dried

2 teaspoons pepper

1 teaspoon salt

½ cup dry white wine

1 cup water

2 pounds fresh peas, shelled

8 large eggs, beaten

⅔ cup grated Parmesan cheese

1 tablespoon chopped parsley

½ teaspoon salt

Pinch of pepper

Salt and pepper, to taste

Place lamb, onion, tomatoes, parsley, basil, pepper, salt, wine and water in a heavy pan on top of stove and simmer, covered, for 1 hour. Meantime, cook fresh peas in enough water to cover them by one inch, for a half hour. In a separate bowl, beat the eggs with the cheese, parsley, salt and pepper and add cooked peas. Place the lamb into a casserole dish and pour the egg mixture and cooked peas over the lamb. Bake for 20 to 30 minutes in a pre-heated 350 degree oven, or until eggs are golden brown. 8 servings.

BALDUCCI FAMILY

Balducci's, in New York's Greenwich Village, is a lush emporium of food that sells moose and mousse, exquisite fruits and vegetables that know no season and fresh delicacies flown in daily from every corner of the globe. This ultimate Mom and Pop shop—a veritable United Nations of both food and shoppers—all began when Pop, Louis Balducci, at the age of 17 became the proud owner of a modest fruit and vegetable stand.

"We enjoy this traditional Italian dish the Monday after Easter Sunday. Whenever possible, we take it to the country-side along with other foods, such as *Foccacia* (a pizza-like bread) and roasted peppers and olives, to celebrate the extended holiday with family and friends."

SPAGHETTI CARBONARA

1/4 pound bacon

1 pound thin spaghetti

4 eggs

1/4 cup heavy cream

1 cup grated Parmesan cheese

1/2 teaspoon salt

1 teaspoon pepper, freshly ground

8 tablespoons butter (1 stick)

Fry the bacon crisply, break into small pieces and set aside. Cook the spaghetti *al dente*, drain and have piping hot at the time the egg, cream and cheese mixture is ready. Put the eggs in a bowl and beat them for a few minutes with a fork. Add the cream, most of the cheese, salt and pepper. Make sure that the mixture is well stirred before it is poured into the hot butter. In a pan or pot large enough to hold the cooked spaghetti, heat the butter until it turns golden, but not brown. Then pour in the egg mixture. Over low heat allow the egg mixture to cook *partially* in the heated butter. Make sure the egg mixture does not cook too much; the hot spaghetti (next step) will complete the cooking process. When the egg mixture is ready, pour in the hot spaghetti and crumbled bacon and stir thoroughly. Keep it over the low heat while stirring. Then serve immediately right from the pan in which the spaghetti and egg mixture were mixed. Serve with the remaining Parmesan cheese. About 6 servings.

JOSEPH CARDINAL BERNARDIN

Archbishop of Chicago, Cardinal Bernardin was born in Columbia, South Carolina. His father was a stonecutter and his mother a seamstress. The Cardinal is a member of the permanent council of the World Synod of Bishops.

The word Carbonara in the title of the recipe comes from the pepper which, grated generously over the top, is thought to resemble charcoal. "As you use this recipe several times, you might decide to alter the amounts of the ingredients a little to suit taste. I hope it works well for you!"

FONDUE BORGHESE

Corn oil (enough to halfway fill 2 meat fondue pots or chafing dishes. For 8 people, 2 pots will be needed to be within reach of all and to maintain the oil's high heat. Candle power is not sufficient.)

Select a combination of meats totaling approximately 4 pounds—to suit all taste preferences.

Cubes of beef and veal

Chicken livers (or calf's liver cut into squares)

2 kinds of sausage

Sauces

Mustard: ½ cup dark mustard blended with 2 tablespoons champagne or dry white wine

Tomato: ½ cup catsup blended with 2 tablespoons Worcestershire sauce and a dash of hot pepper sauce

Mayonnaise: ½ cup mayonnaise blended with 2 tablespoons fresh lemon juice

Sour cream: ½ cup sour cream blended with 1 tablespoon chopped capers plus 1 teaspoon caper juice

Yoghurt: ½ cup yoghurt blended with 1 tablespoon minced onion

Give each guest a portion of each sauce so that they may dip to their heart's content. Scallop or other sea shells make excellent containers for the sauces. Fill two open chafing dishes halfway with oil. (Sprinkle a few grains of raw rice in the pans to prevent oil from sparkling.) When a twist of Italian bread dropped into the hot oil browns in a minute, the temperature is correct. Bring the chafing dishes to the table, keeping the fire on underneath. Place them so that they are within reach of all. Using fondue forks, each guest cooks a choice of meat in the heated oil. Serves 8.

PRINCESS MARCELLA BORGHESE

Princess Marcella Borghese, creator of the famous line of cosmetics, and Prince Paolo are the parents of twin sons who have presented them with five grandchildren—all avid young skiers. This is a favorite family recipe often served for luncheon. All members of the family enjoy the "coziness" evoked by this dish and the Princess promises, "the same atmosphere of warmth and conviviality will extend to all families." The Borghese manner is to serve it with a hot, crusty loaf of bread and an assortment of cheese and fruit. A warm pudding or a chestnut torte is a traditional capping to the meal—and then back off to the ski slopes.

MARIO BUATTA

He DOES do windows—and walls and furniture—and this interior designer's clients include Henry Ford II, the Winterthur Museum galleries and the Metropolitan Opera House offices. Turn the pages of any interior design magazine, and rooms with his "The Un-Decorated Look" will catch your eye.

"I suggest making Bagna Cauda on payday when you can buy with reckless abandon the most virginal possible olive oil."

BAGNA CAUDA

½ cup medium cream
4 tablespoons butter
2 garlic cloves, finely minced
½ cup olive oil
8 anchovy fillets chopped
Fresh Vegetables—an assortment of crisp dipping-sized vegetables which may include: fennel, carrots, celery, scallions, broccoli and cauliflower, peppers and zucchini.

In a heavy saucepan, bring the cream to a boil. Turn down the heat and cook it, stirring frequently, until it has reduced and thickened. While the cream is simmering, heat the butter in a skillet. When it foams, sauté the garlic in it lightly. Stir in the oil. Add the anchovies and with a wooden spoon mash them until they form a paste. Slowly add the oil and butter mixture to the cream, stirring constantly. Transfer to a container—preferably earthenware—that will set over a candle warmer. (If mixture separates, stir a few drops of additional cream into it to smooth it.) Serve with the vegetables for dipping. Serves 6.

PAOLO BUITONI

The Buitoni food empire started in 1827, when Matriarch Giulia Buitoni pawned her wedding jewels and used the money to start a small macaroni business. History repeated itself in 1939 when a later Mrs. B., visiting this country, was prevented by the outbreak of war from returning to Italy. Once again, jewels were pawned and another Buitoni pasta plant was born. So popular was the product that a restaurant opened on Broadway where 25 cents, paid at a turnstile, entitled customers to all the spaghetti they could eat from a conveyor belt counter rolling straight out from the kitchen.

Paolo Buitoni, as president of another family business, Perugina Chocolates, holds what may be the sweetest job in the world.

SANFATUCCHIO T-BONE STEAK

"I own a farm in Sanfatucchio, a small village on the border of the Trasimeno Lake at the extreme south of Tuscany. There I raise cattle: French breeds— Limousins, Charolais, Garonnais; and Italian breeds—Chianina, Marchigiana. The meat of these animals is different from the American meat in the sense that it is not marbled. Instead, it is lean internally, and it is covered by a thick fat cover. My recipe results in an outstanding steak, if the meat comes from an animal of Southern-European breed. I understand that quality butchers carry such meat because a small number of American cattle-raising farmers have imported French-bred animals. If you decide to go for this recipe, be sure to get meat which is not marbled. The steaks should be 2½ inches thick, with bone left attached. Be also sure that at least 15 days have passed since the animal has been slaughtered, if fresh; or else that it has been properly frozen. Prepare the steaks by rubbing the meat lightly on both sides with a crushed garlic clove, and peppering it both sides with freshly crushed black pepper. You will also rub the steaks vigorously with a handful of rosemary leaves. Have a barbecue ready. It is essential to have a very hot setting because the meat should cook instantly outside, so as to steam inside. I obtain my best results using dry good oak wood and adding some wood coal. Place the steaks on the barbecue, allowing five inches between the meat surface and the embers. Allow 5 to 6 minutes for each side, and move the cooked steaks to a hot dish. Give salt to the steaks at your taste, and season with extra-quality Italian olive oil. I am confident that you are not going to be deceived."

NICOLA BULGARI

The family's shops, located in New York, Rome, Geneva, Monte Carlo and Paris, carry jewels that bear the Greek-lettered BVLGARI stamp. Though surrounded by such baubles as a necklace of rare pigeon's blood rubies worth a king's ransom, Nicola Bulgari wears only a gold wedding band.

"I usually consider Risotto a main course because we are not meat eaters. With this we have a choice of cheeses and we allow ourselves to indulge on desserts. A favorite of ours is chocolate cake—almost like a giant brownie—with raspberry sauce."

SPRING RISOTTO

2 small yellow onions

1 stalk celery

2 small carrots

1 bunch parsley

5 to 6 basil leaves (do not wash)

8 plum tomatoes (scald and remove skins)

2 small zucchini

Hot water (as needed, about 2 quarts)

2 teaspoons salt

2 bouillon cubes (optional)

3 ounces blanched bacon (4 strips)

1/3 cup olive oil

2 cups shelled fresh peas

18 ounces rice (Italian arborio preferred)

Parmesan cheese, to taste

Clean and coarsely chop onions, celery, carrots, parsley, basil and combine. Chop tomatoes (discard seeds and hard portions) and zucchini but hold them aside. Put water on fire, add salt and bouillon cubes and bring to a boil. Cut bacon into small strips. Put it into pan over medium flame, make it crisp, then drain off fat. Add oil and vegetables except zucchini, tomatoes and peas. When onion is golden, add the reserved vegetables and cook on a medium fire for 20 minutes. Add rice, stir, let it absorb the liquid, then add more liquid always stirring until rice has lost its starchy flavor. The whole process will take about 30 minutes. Remove from fire and add Parmesan cheese. BUON APPETITO! Serves 8.

THE CELEBRATED PASTA OF ITALY

Margaret and G. Franco Romagnoli, the owners of two restaurants called The Romagnoli's Table—one in The Faneuil Hall Marketplace in Boston and the other in The Mall in Burlington, Massachusetts—are also the authors of three cookbooks on Italian cookery, the latest being *The New Italian Cooking*. Mrs. Romagnoli says,

"Pasta, once identified with Italy only, has jumped all ethnical barriers and become international. Absolute simplicity or extravagant elegance, what a good dish pasta really is: not mere sustenance for the body, but food for the soul, a lift to the spirit. Ah, pasta!"

In his 65-page manuscript, "Libro De Arte Coquinaria," Maestro Martino, chef to a priest of Lucullan tastes, wrote down the world's first pasta recipe. The year was believed to be 1450. The recipe, titled Sicilian Macaroni, called for fine white flour mixed with egg white and rose water. These ingredients were to be made into a dough "nice and

Margaret and G. Franco Romagnoli

hard" and rolled into a log. A long iron rod was then pushed firmly into the log; when removed, the result was tube-shaped pasta. If dried in the sun, Chef Martino promised, it would last for two or three years—especially if made during the August moon. And, naturally, he specified that the macaroni be served with grated cheese.

Although the tale persists that Marco Polo first introduced pasta to the western world when he brought back samples from China, historians believe that pasta was a food common to the Romans. No matter who invented pasta, the variety of shapes, the sauces, the treatments, the absolute outpouring of invention lavished upon pasta by the Italians make it their national treasure. And ever

since the nineteenth century wave of Italian immigrants arrived here, pasta has been a mainstay of the American diet.

Basically, there are two kinds of pasta—dried and fresh—but there are hundreds of variations on the theme. One encyclopedia states that there are 347 forms of pasta. Here are just a few of them:

Angel hair—the finest form of pasta

Cappelletti—little hats

Conchiglie—seashells

Farfalle—bow ties

Fettuccine—ribbons

Fusilli—spirals

Gemelli—twin strands, twisted

Lasagna—wide squares

Linguine—flat, narrow with tapered edges

Manicotti—muffs for stuffing

Nidi—nests

Orecchiette—little ears

Penne—shaped like a quill pen

Tortellini—navel-shaped

COLD STRIPED BASS WITH PESTO VINAIGRETTE

Vinaigrette Sauce

¾ cup olive oil

3-4 tablespoons wine vinegar or fresh lemon juice
  or a combination

1 teaspoon salt

½ teaspoon pepper

½ teaspoon dry mustard

Place the ingredients in a jar. Cover and shake until blended.
Taste and correct seasoning if necessary.

4 filets of bass (about 8 ounces each)

½ celery stalk

½ carrot

½ small red onion

1 sprig parsley

Salt and pepper, to taste

2 teaspoons Pesto Sauce (See Bill Fugazy's recipe)

1 cup Vinaigrette Sauce (Above)

2 plum tomatoes, chopped

Poach the bass covered in a small amount of water with the
celery, carrot, onion, parsley, salt and pepper. (Allow about 6
minutes for each inch of thickness.) Remove from heat and allow to
cool to room temperature. Combine the Pesto, Vinaigrette and
tomatoes. To serve, place the fish on a platter and pour the tomato
mixture over it. Serves 4.

LEO CASTELLI

Combining the Italian "eye for art" with
a gift for discovering artists in their chrysalis,
he developed an incomparable stable of American
artists. A visit to his SoHo gallery is like a visit
to the Museum of Modern Art with paintings
by Jasper Johns, Andy Warhol, Robert
Rauschenberg, and Frank Stella at every turn.

As the Bleecker Street Ristorante da
Silvano is one of his favorite haunts, he asked
the owner to share his recipe. "This recipe is not
very complicated, but the way it's done by
Silvano is just perfect. As always, the quality of
the product and the care taken in going through
the various steps are what count."

29

GOVERNOR AND MRS. RICHARD F. CELESTE

From the Governor's mansion in Ohio comes a recipe that has long been a family favorite—especially of their youngest child, Stephen. They caution that it takes a little time to make, but "it's worth it." The Celestes stress that the seafood should be fresh. For that reason, lobster was substituted for the crab which was not at height of season.

HOMEMADE FETTUCCINI WITH FRESH SEAFOOD

Pasta

2¼ to 2½ cup all-purpose flour

⅓ cup water

2 eggs

1 egg yolk

1 tablespoon olive oil or salad oil

1 teaspoon salt

In a large bowl combine one cup of the flour with the water, eggs, egg yolk, oil and salt. With electric mixer set at low speed, beat 2 minutes. With wooden spoon, stir in enough additional flour to make a soft dough. Turn dough onto lightly-floured surface, knead it until smooth and elastic—about 10 minutes. Cover dough and let rest 30 minutes. On floured surface, roll out dough as thin as possible. Fold, cut into 1/8-inch strips and place them in a single layer on clean cloth towels. Let air dry 2 hours before cooking.

Basic Alfredo Sauce

4 tablespoons butter, melted

¼ cup grated Parmesan cheese

¼ cup grated Romano cheese

½ cup Half and Half

Salt and pepper, to taste

Combine above ingredients and set aside.

Fresh scallops, shrimp and crab (¼ to ⅓ pound of each)

Butter

1 clove garlic

Juice of ½ lemon

¼ cup dry white wine

Parsley, chopped very fine

Sauté scallops, shrimp and crab in butter with garlic clove until done. Squeeze in lemon juice. Add wine and cook at high heat for about 3 minutes. Add Alfredo sauce mixture and cook at low heat for 3 to 5 minutes, then toss in cooked noodles. Place on warm dish and top with fresh parsley. Serves 6.

ZUCCHINI AND GREEN RICE

1½ pounds zucchini

2 cups cooked brown rice

Juice of 1 lemon

¾ cup chopped parsley

1 teaspoon salt

Pinch of pepper

1 teaspoon dried basil

2 tablespoons oil

1 cup low-fat cottage cheese

½ cup grated Cheddar cheese

2 tablespoons grated Parmesan cheese

Slice zucchini in ¼-inch rounds. Steam until done but still firm. Preheat oven to 350 degrees. Mix rice with lemon juice, parsley, salt, pepper and basil. Rub oil inside baking dish. In it layer rice mixture, cottage cheese and zucchini. Top with Cheddar cheese. Bake uncovered for 10 to 15 minutes. Sprinkle with Parmesan cheese. Serves 4 to 6.

JAMES COCO

No fewer than 20 years of struggle brought Coco the overnight stardom he had dreamed of while attending movies as a boy in the Bronx. His portrayal of the lead in Neil Simon's *Last of the Red Hot Lovers* in 1969 put his name in lights. He went on to play Sancho Panza in *Man of La Mancha* with Sophia Loren. He continues to receive top billing with his best-seller, *The James Coco Diet Book.*

"A favorite recipe of mine. It's great to serve at card games or informal buffets."

ONION, WINE AND SAUSAGE SAUCE WITH POLENTA

The Sauce

5 large Bermuda or Spanish Onions

2 pounds Italian sweet sausage

1 cup red wine

Salt and pepper to taste

Grated cheese

Chop onions and place in large sauce pot. Add water midway up the onions. Simmer onions, uncovered, about 15 minutes. Meanwhile, prick sausages, then boil them a short while to remove fat. Brown sausages in a skillet, then add them with the wine to the onions. Add salt and pepper to taste. Simmer from 30 to 45 minutes.

The Polenta

1½ quarts boiling water

2 teaspoons salt

2 medium potatoes, peeled, sliced very thin

1 pound yellow cornmeal

In heavy pot, add sliced potatoes to the salted, boiling water. When water comes to boil again, use a wooden spoon to stir in cornmeal. (Some cooks like to moisten cornmeal using a little additional cold water before stirring into pot to prevent lumps.) Continue cooking and stirring for 30 minutes or until cornmeal leaves the side of the pot easily. Turn out onto large platter. Serve on individual plates. Spoon Onion and Sausage Sauce over top. Serve with a bowl of freshly grated cheese. Serves 4-6.

PERRY COMO

Born Pierino Como, the seventh son of a seventh son, by age 14 he had his own barbershop. In 1937, he began singing with the Ted Weems Orchestra and soon sang his way straight into the heart of America via RCA Victor recordings, 20th Century Fox movies and a weekly tv show. Legions of fans turned his recordings of "Prisoner of Love," "Temptation" and "'Til the End of Time" into jukebox hits but Perry, in inimitable laid-back style, confesses, "I'd rather play golf."

Of his Polenta recipe Perry says, "This dish was very special to the whole family as I was growing up and it's still a big favorite."

VEAL SPEDINI TERMINI

1 pound veal, cut for Spedini (3-inch squares)
1 32-ounce can crushed tomatoes
2 cups breadcrumbs
½ cup grated Locatelli cheese or Parmesan cheese
6 sprigs parsley, chopped
1½ cups corn oil, divided
¼ pound imported Fontina cheese, cut into 1-inch pieces
2 medium onions, sliced
12 bay leaves

Marinate the veal squares in crushed tomatoes overnight or at least 2 hours before preparing. Combine
breadcrumbs with cheese and chopped parsley in a bowl.
In a frying pan, put 1 cup of the oil and toast the breadcrumb mixture until golden. Set aside to cool. Pour
remaining ½ cup of oil in bottom of a 13 by 9-inch baking
dish, coating entire bottom of pan. Coat each Spedini
on both sides with toasted breadcrumb mixture. (Reserve
the tomatoes.) Place a piece of Fontina cheese in the center
of each Spedini. Overlap opposite sides over cheese. Place
Spedini in baking dish in rows and top each with an
onion slice and a bay leaf. Spread the reserved crushed
tomatoes over the top. Bake at 375 degrees for 30 minutes.
Don't overcook. Serves 4-6.

GOVERNOR AND
MRS. MARIO CUOMO

Before moving to the Governor's mansion in Albany,
the Cuomos raised their five children in a neighborhood in
Queens where the streets are named Romeo, Nero, Pompeii
and Palermo. The Governor, formerly adjunct professor at
his alma mater, the Law School of St. John's University,
is the author of the blockbuster best-seller *Diaries of
Mario M. Cuomo.*

37

PINK EGGS

Fresh zucchini
Oil and butter
Leftover tomato sauce
Eggs, lightly beaten
Butter

Slice zucchini and saute in a little oil and butter. Meanwhile, in a saucepan, heat leftover tomato sauce. When zucchini is transparent, add to tomato sauce. Melt a little butter in a skillet, put in the beaten eggs and start scrambling with the right hand. With the left hand, add the heated tomato sauce mixture. Continue scrambling and cook to taste.

KITTY D'ALESSIO

The stylish, sophisticated president of Chanel says, "I adore Italian food and I subscribe to a spoonful of pasta a day. But I'm a disaster in the kitchen and a disgrace to the good cooking tradition of my family. Both my sweet, darling mother and my grandmother had the unique talent of being able to create a feast to feed an unexpected, but genuinely welcomed, crowd in a matter of moments—and out of what seemed like one egg and leftover tomato sauce."

Reminiscing about an almost-forgotten nursery food, Pink Eggs, she says: "Grandmother often served these to me as a special Saturday snack. She believed that the eggs should be beaten gently but well—best accomplished by 'running them through a fork.'"

39

POLLO ALL'UVA

(Chicken with Grapes)

2 tablespoons butter

2 tablespoons olive oil

2 small frying chickens, quartered
  or 4 cornish hens, halved

1 tablespoon flour

2 teaspoons salt

½ teaspoon freshly ground pepper

2 cups dry white wine, divided

¼ cup juniper berries, crushed (or 2 bay leaves)

½ cup chicken broth

1 cup green grapes, halved if large

Heat the butter and oil in a frying pan and saute the chicken until lightly browned. Remove chicken from pan and sprinkle drippings with flour, salt and pepper and stir until flour dissolves. Place the chicken and pan drippings in a roasting pan. Add 1 cup of the wine and the juniper berries or bay leaves and bake, uncovered, for 30 minutes at 350 degrees. Lower the oven temperature to 300 degrees and add the remaining cup of wine, broth and grapes. Continue baking 30 minutes or until the juice runs clear when the thigh is pierced with a fork. Serves 4.

ALAN D'AMBROSIO

As the publisher of the magazine *ATTENZIONE,* the senior partner of a law firm, and the president of a fashion manufacturing and importing company, he divides his time between Rome, New York, and Central America. Despite this hectic schedule, he finds time for organizations that promote Italian culture and heritage.

And he cooks, too. "This recipe is based upon a Tuscan recipe for preparing pheasant. If desired, the grapes may be first peeled and soaked in brandy."

MOTHER DEBARTOLO'S PITZALES

3 cups flour

¾ cups vegetable shortening or lard

3 eggs

¾ cups sugar

Grated rind of 1 lemon

1 teaspoon anise seed

Confectionery sugar

In a large shallow bowl use pastry blender or hands to work flour and shortening together to the consistency of coarse meal. Set aside in refrigerator or cool place. Beat eggs until fluffy and creamy, then add sugar and mix well. Stir in lemon rind and anise seeds. Blend the egg mixture into the flour mixture slowly and gently, being careful not to work the dough too much. Chill dough for an hour. Roll into 1-inch balls. Place each ball in hot Pitzale or waffle iron. Press flat and bake until golden brown. Cool on rack. Sprinkle with confectionery sugar. Makes 48.

EDWARD J. DEBARTOLO, SR. AND EDWARD J. DEBARTOLO, JR.

A graduate of Notre Dame, Edward De Bartolo, Senior, as a young army engineer, returned from Pacific combat without a dime in his pocket, but built a shopping center empire. The enclosed malls he owns and operates stretch from coast to coast, making him one of the nation's largest landlords. His son, a chip off the old block, is the owner of the San Francisco '49ers.

"This is Mother De Bartolo's recipe for Pitzales. Every week until she died at age 89, she baked and had delivered to my office far too many Pitzales. They arrived beautifully arranged in a large, flat basket covered with a hand-embroidered linen tea towel. Her secret was the use of anise seed instead of anise oil and freshly grated lemon peel. The flavor and texture were like no other. She was a treasure."

THE CELEBRATED DOLCI OF ITALY

Marcella Hazan

Marcella Hazan is a famous cook whose schools in Venice and Bologna, Italy, are as well known as her books, *The Classic Italian Cookbook* and *More Classic Italian Cooking*. Her forthcoming book, *Good Italian Cooking*, will also be published by Knopf.

"Italian desserts and pastries are to other sweets as champagne is to wine. They carry with them the uplifting spirit of celebration. From the mid-morning espresso break to a feast day dinner, any occasion of which they are part is an occasion to cheer about."

Dolci. Is there a word in any other language that sounds so sweet and describes so well a special category of food? *Dolci* —as in *La Dolce Vita* — brings to mind Catherine De Medici arriving as a bride in France with her entourage of pastry chefs. *Dolci* suggests confections so entwined in the traditions of a special festival that they are baked only on that one day each year. *Dolce* means an afternoon pause at an umbrella-topped table for a dish of *granita di caffe* — ice made from a sweet brew of espresso coffee.

This universal fondness for sweetness should not surprise—it was the spice-trading merchants of Venice who first introduced sugar to the western world. And in a culture infused with painting and tapestry, with sculpture and architecture, it is not likely that the bakers would pass by an opportunity to express their heritage in a sweet state of excess. This love of embellishment reached a peak in the centerpieces called Triumphs for the Table, which were great statues of spun sugar and marzipan. When a seventeenth century pope entertained Queen Christina of Sweden, the centerpiece was a model of a seaport with edible buildings, piers, ships and even live fish swimming in the harbor.

When we consider that the classic French cake *Genoise* was named after the city of its origin, Genoa, we appreciate the long tradition of pastry making that exists in Italy. The Genoise cake serves often as a mere starting point. It may be dressed with rum or liqueur, candied fruit or nuts or chocolate cream—or all of the above.

The pastry cooks' guild was formed the year Christopher Columbus was discovering America, and so they have had centuries to perfect their edible artifacts. Frequently they focused on feast days. For Christmas there is *Panettone*, a rich yeast cake studded with fruit. Easter favorites are the Neapolitan specialty *Pastiera* or *Cassatta*, the ornate cake from Sicily. Cookies, too, mark celebrations. *Zeppole di San Giuseppe* are fritters, often cinnamon-flavored, that honor Saint Joseph. For St. Martin's Day, the cookies are baked in the shape of a knight on horseback, while bone-shaped cookies appear on The Day of the Dead (All Saint's Day). Confections have their symbolism also. The sugared almonds showered upon brides and grooms are the same token as the rice thrown in America.

Fie on the idea that a fig and a piece of cheese are the extent of Italian desserts!

VEAL SCALLOPINI

3 pounds veal round (sliced thin)
¼ cup flour
Salt and pepper
4 tablespoons olive oil (approximately)
3 medium onions, finely chopped (less, if preferred)
2 sprigs parsley, chopped
½ cup white wine (Sauterne)
1 can mushrooms (4 ounces)

Cut veal into 2-inch pieces. Shake in flour. Season with salt and pepper. Heat oil in a large skillet and brown veal in it. Add onions and parsley and stir until onions brown. Add mushrooms with their liquid, plus a little water. Cover tightly and cook over low heat for 1 hour. (If mixture is not brown enough, add Kitchen Bouquet.) Add wine a half hour before done to avoid evaporation. Serves 6.

SENATOR DENNIS DECONCINI

A native of Tucson, Arizona, he was elected to the United States Senate in 1976 and is a member of two of its most powerful committees—Appropriations and Judiciary.

His bride, Susan DeConcini, started married life with the realization that the only thing she could really cook was chocolate chip cookies—so she turned to her mother-in-law for help. This recipe—the Senator's favorite—was the result.

45

LASAGNA VERDE
(Green Lasagna)

Bolognese Sauce

1 tablespoon butter
Olive oil
½ onion, chopped
¼ stalk celery, chopped
1 carrot, chopped
1 bay leaf
¾ pound ground beef
½ cup strong red wine
2 tablespoons tomato paste
½ pound tomatoes, skinned
Salt and pepper to taste

Melt the butter in a saucepan. Add a little olive oil. Add the onion, celery, carrot and bay leaf. Cook and stir until brown. Add ground beef. Cook and stir until meat is done. Then pour in the wine and let it evaporate. Add tomato paste, stir for a few minutes, then pour the tomatoes into the mixture and stir. Add salt and pepper to taste. Let the sauce cook over a low fire for 2 hours, stirring occasionally to avoid sticking.

Bechamel Sauce

6 tablespoons butter
6 tablespoons flour
3 cups milk, warmed
Salt to taste
Ground nutmeg

1 pound green lasagna noodles
Grated Parmesan Reggiano

Melt the butter in a saucepan. Add the flour, mixing it thoroughly for a few minutes. Then slowly pour the warm milk into the mixture, stirring to avoid curdling. Cook for another 5 minutes Add salt and a pinch of ground nutmeg. In salted water, with a little oil, cook the green lasagna noodles. Remove *al dente*, pour cold water over them and drain very well. Grease the baking dish. Lay the lasagna in rows, pour some Bechamel Sauce, then Bolognese Sauce, and sprinkle a handful of cheese. Repeat the procedure for each layer. Top the last layer with more Bechamel and a few drops of Bolognese. Sprinkle the top with cheese. Put in the oven at 350 degrees for 15 minutes. Serves 6.

DINO DE LAURENTIIS

By age 21, this renowned impresario had formed his own film company. In partnership with Carlo Ponti he produced the films of Fellini and Rossellini. *War and Peace, Bitter Rice, La Strada,* and *King Kong* are just some of his big pictures. Ever the showman, he opened in New York the DDL Food Show—an extravaganza of good sight, good smell, and good taste.

"The secret of fine cooking is this: one must cook with love."

GREAT-GREAT NONNA CONCETTA'S SECRET PIE

Italian Cream Filling

(To be made in advance. It must be cooled and may be prepared the night before.)

1 quart milk

1 cup light cream

1 teaspoon arrowroot or 1 tablespoon cornstarch

12 egg yolks

1 cup sugar

Rinds of 2 lemons (not grated)

Place the milk and cream in top of double boiler. Stir in the arrowroot or cornstarch until smooth. Add the egg yolks, sugar and lemon rinds and place over hot water. Stir slowly, always in one direction (if not, it will curdle). Stir until thick, then remove from heat. Discard the lemons—the cook gets to lick them—and let filling cool.

Pastry Crust

3 eggs

¾ cup sugar

¾ cup peanut oil

Juice from half a lemon

Juice from half an orange

Pinch of salt

1 generous, heaping teaspoon baking powder

Flour, as needed (about 3 cups)

One layer of ladyfingers, stale

Cherries from 1 jar of preserves

Beat eggs in a large bowl. Add sugar, oil, lemon, and orange juice, salt and baking powder and mix. Add as much flour as needed to form dough. Set aside about one-third to use for tarts. (See cooks' comments.) Divide remaining dough and roll out for top and bottom crusts. Place one in a 10-inch deep-dish pie pan. On it arrange a layer of ladyfingers. Top with the cream filling. Empty the jar of cherry preserves onto a plate and dot the cream filling with whole cherries. (Return the remainder to jar and re-label "cherry jelly.") Top with other crust, pinching edges to seal. Bake in preheated 350 degree oven until good and brown—about 1 hour. Cool before serving. 8 to 10 servings.

JERRY DELLA FEMINA AND RON TRAVISANO

Madison Avenue's buttoned down, grey flannel image has not been the same since these two rebels in boots, beards, and jeans founded their trend-setting advertising agency. Typical of their fresh approach was their tv commercial featuring Yogi Berra as "One of those sissies who uses his wife's hair spray."

By mutual agreement, they provided this recipe from Ron's Great-Great-Grandmother. "This recipe for the pastry crust makes too much for one pie. Rather than reducing the quantities we like to encourage cooks to use it to make a dozen lemon meringue tarts for the sake of all that unwanted egg white and lemon juice."

PISTACHIO CAKE

1 white or yellow cake mix

2 boxes pistachio instant pudding mix

½ cup oil

½ cup warm water

½ cup milk

5 eggs

½ cup poppy seeds (optional)

Blend all ingredients in a large bowl. Beat about 2 minutes. Pour into greased and floured bundt or tube pan and bake for 45 to 50 minutes in pre-heated 350 degree oven.

Frosting

1 cup heavy cream

1 box pistachio instant pudding mix.

1 tablespoon white *creme de menthe* (optional)

Beat all ingredients together in a bowl. Frost cooled cake. 10 servings.

DOM DELUISE

A child of the Big Apple, he attended the famous "Fame" school—The High School for the Performing Arts. He is known as one of the most inventive of the "new generation" comics and is a frequent talk show guest—especially on Johnny Carson's show. His portrayal of Buddy Bizarre in Mel Brooks' *Blazing Saddles* is a classic.

"Cooking is one of my favorite hobbies and I look forward to adding this book to my cookbook collection."

DOM DIMAGGIO

The youngest of the famous baseball-playing DiMaggio brothers, he was known as "The Little Professor." Though he was raised in California, he made his reputation in baseball as the star of an eastern team, the Boston Red Sox. Nowadays, his catch of the day is likely to be at DiMaggio's Restaurant on Fisherman's Wharf in San Francisco.

ZABAGLIONED STRAWBERRIES

1 quart whole, perfect strawberries

6 egg yolks

2 tablespoons sugar

2 tablespoons *amaretto* liqueur

½ cup medium cream

Rinse the strawberries and set them aside to drain dry or pat dry with paper towels. Hull. Put the egg yolks and sugar in a round-bottomed mixing bowl. With a whisk or portable electric mixer beat until pale in color and thick. Set bowl over a pot of hot water. (Do not let the water boil or touch the bowl.) Place over medium heat and continue to beat the egg mixture. When the mixture becomes very thick, remove from heat and stir in the *amaretto*. Set the bowl into a larger bowl containing ice and stir frequently to hasten cooling. In another bowl whip the cream. When the custard has cooled to room temperature, stir in the whipped cream. Distribute strawberries into 6 large wine or sherbet glasses. Drench with the Zabaglione Sauce and serve. 6 servings. If refrigerated, sauce will thicken into a pudding. An alternate serving suggestion is to pour the freshly-prepared Zabaglione into stemmed glasses and refrigerate. This will make 4 half-cup servings.

HOW TO BOIL WATER *(Editors' Note)*

Without a doubt, the best reason for boiling water is to prepare pasta. Here follow definitive directions:

Start with a big pot and a large quantity of water. Use about 4 quarts of water to each pound of dry pasta. Add 1 teaspoon of salt for every quart of water. Salt raises the water's boiling point (boiling salted water is hotter than unsalted boiling water), so the pasta cooks more quickly. The salt will also flavor the pasta. When the water is boiling vigorously—some call it angrily—add the pasta. Stir once with a wooden spoon to separate strands and loosen any that stick to the bottom of the pot. Cover the pot with a "cracked lid," so that the water will quickly return to a boil. Remove lid and stir again. Cook only until *al dente* which can be best determined by biting into a single strand. For dried or commercial pasta, begin to check at 7 minutes. For fresh pasta as little as 1 minute may suffice. Immediately drain into a colander. Rinse only if it is to be used for cold salad.

JOE DIMAGGIO

Since he grew up on the San Francisco waterfront, it is not surprising that his first baseball bat was a broken oar. He played center field for the New York Yankees and did it with such style and grace, he was dubbed the "Yankee Clipper." Mountains of bubble gum have been chewed by youngsters searching for the baseball trading card picturing their idol, a baseball legend. "I love Italian cooking. I love Italian food. I eat it all the time, but I can't boil water."

SENATOR
PETE DOMENICI

After graduating from the University of New Mexico, he signed on as a minor league pitcher, then taught junior high math before entering law. When he ran for the Senate in 1972, he was the first successful Republican candidate from New Mexico in 38 years. Chairman of the Senate Budget Committee, he has been called by the press, "a godsend," a "stubborn spirit," and "a refreshing break from the mania on Capitol Hill."

WILD DUCK DOMENICI

6 wild ducks, preferably from New Mexico skies

3 apples, cut in wedges

3 onions—2 cut in wedges; one finely diced

3 packages dry gravy mix (brown)

2 teaspoons salt

Pepper

½ cup flour

6 tablespoons lemon juice concentrate

6 tablespoons orange marmalade

2 6-ounce cans frozen orange juice,
    thawed but undiluted

¾ cup white wine (optional)

1½ cups hot water

3 oven cooking bags

Thoroughly wash duck; wipe dry inside and out. Sprinkle duck cavities with salt and pepper. Place apple and onion wedges in each duck. Combine gravy mix, flour, salt, lemon and orange juices and stir to dissolve flour. Stir in marmalade, wine (if desired), the reserved diced onion and the hot water. Arrange two ducks in each oven cooking bag; divide the liquid among the three bags and seal according to instructions. Place in roasting pan and cut two or three slits in top of each bag. Bake at 350 degrees for 2½ hours. Serve ducks with pan gravy and wild rice to 12 or 14 good eaters!

MANICOTTI

"You'll need tomato sauce as you get to the final step of preparation for baking. I make a 'from scratch' Bolognese meat sauce (my family is spoiled) and I make a lot. So what I don't use on the Manicotti, I save. You can use any of the prepared sauces—start out with one jar, if you need another, use the second."

Pancakes

1 cup flour

1 cup water

¼ teaspoon salt

4 eggs

Combine flour, water and salt and beat until smooth. Beat in the eggs *one at a time*. Heat a 5 to 6-inch skillet and grease with a few drops of oil. Put about 3 tablespoons batter in hot skillet and roll around pan to distribute evenly. Cook over low heat until firm. *Do not brown*. Turn and cook lightly on other side. (Do not grease skillet a second time.) Makes 12 to 14 pancakes.

Filling

½ teaspoon salt

3 eggs

2 pounds ricotta cheese

Pepper to taste

1 pound mozzarella, cut in strips

Mix the salt, eggs, ricotta cheese, Parmesan cheese and pepper together for the filling. Put about 2 tablespoons of the mixture and a strip of mozzarella on each pancake and roll up. Pour your tomato sauce on the bottom of a large shallow baking dish (just to cover). Put pancakes seam side down in dish. Cover with more sauce and sprinkle with additional grated cheese. Bake in 350 degree oven for 45 minutes. (The pancakes may be made the day before and refrigerated. On serving day, just fill and bake. If pancakes are made the day before, put wax paper between each to prevent sticking.) Serve with additional sauce and grated cheese, to add according to individual taste. Serves 6-8.

CONGRESSWOMAN GERALDINE A. FERRARO

She is the first woman selected to run for Vice President of the United States on a major party ticket. A former teacher and assistant District Attorney, she has served in Congress as a New York City representative for six years.

"This recipe is time consuming but well worth it. If followed carefully, you will have the best Manicotti this side of the Atlantic."

57

WILLIAM FUGAZY

The Fugazy fleet of limousines, buses, and vans placed bumper to bumper could circle the globe—and does. His conglomerate traces its roots back to the Greenwich Village travel service founded in the 1800's by his grandfather. From the sporting world to Hollywood, this entrepreneur travels in celebrity circles, so it was fitting that he provided transportation for Pope Paul's trip to New York.

"Pesto is truly a sauce created by the Genoese. It is one of the simplest and most fragrant dishes you will ever try."

PESTO SAUCE
(Genoese Basil Sauce)

1½ cups fresh basil,
   firmly packed

½ cup fresh parsley,
   firmly packed

½ cup pine nuts

3 garlic cloves, lightly crushed

1 cup olive oil

½ cup Parmesan cheese,
   freshly grated

Salt to taste

2 tablespoons hot water

Put basil, parsley, pine nuts and garlic in blender. With motor running on high speed add the oil slowly and blend until smooth. When the ingredients are evenly blended, pour into a bowl and beat in cheese by hand. Add salt to taste. Before serving the Pesto Sauce over pasta, add the hot water to the sauce. You will find this makes the blending of the pesto with the pasta a little easier. Serves 6.

HEDY GIUSTI-LANHAM

She is the petite, blonde Venetian known for her wit and charm and for her guidance of the America-Italy Society. She is the founder of the *Scuola Italiana di Cucina* and is the author of the award-winning book, *The Cuisine of Venice*.

RISOTTO CON MOZZARELLA AFFUMICATA
(Risotto with Smoked Mozzarella)

2 quarts broth, chicken or beef or mixture of both
1 stick butter
1 pound Italian rice (see below)
1 slice smoked mozzarella about 1 inch thick (see below)
Pinch of salt, if desired
Freshly ground pepper to taste

Bring the broth to a boil and keep it simmering. In a sturdy saucepan melt half the butter and add the rice. Stir with a wooden spoon until the rice is well-coated and glistening. Add two ladles of broth and continue stirring over medium heat. As the rice absorbs the broth add more broth a little at a time. The rice should never be completely submerged but should also not be allowed to dry completely. After about 10 minutes try a grain of rice between your teeth. Careful! Nothing is hotter than boiling rice. It should be half done. Cut the mozzarella into chunks and add to the rice stirring briskly. The cheese will melt into the rice. After a total of 20 minutes cooking time, taste again and add salt and pepper, if desired. Add half of the remaining butter and stir. Risotto should be done. Heat a platter that is large enough to hold the Risotto with a wide rim to spare. Spoon the Risotto onto it, place the last tablespoons of butter on top. Serve immediately, so the butter will run onto the rice. Serves 6 as first course or as a light luncheon.

"Italian rice is available in most supermarkets and in all specialty stores. It is shorter and thicker than Carolina rice and a must for Risotto, just as Carolina rice is a must for pilau.

"There are two smoked mozzarellas on the market. One is round, moist and frequently made by the store that sells it. The other is commercially packaged and comes in squares about four inches by four inches. It is much harder than the fresh variety, but it will do if the fresh mozzarella is not available. In either case the brown rind should not be discarded: it is part of the cheese. Mozzarella is slightly salty and requires very little, or no, additional salt.

"Be sure not to serve Risotto in a deep bowl. When heaped in a mound, the rice continues to cook and gets overdone. Rice should be *al dente*, meaning the grains should be biteable and separate, held together by the creamy substance of cheese and butter. In northern Italy this dish is more popular than pasta."

TORTA DI CASTAGNE

(Fresh Chestnut Torte)

2 pounds fresh chestnuts

Coarse grained salt

½ teaspoon fennel seeds

3 tablespoons sweet butter

7 eggs

1 cup granulated sugar

3 tablespoons confectionery sugar

Soak chestnuts overnight in large bowl of cold water. Bring a large stockpot of salted water to a boil, then add drained soaked chestnuts and fennel seeds. Boil until chestnuts are completely cooked (about 2 hours). While still hot, remove shells and skin from the chestnuts and pass them through a food mill into a large bowl. Melt butter in top of double boiler over hot water and let cool for about 10 minutes. Add cooled butter to the chestnut puree and mix well with wooden spoon. Separate four of the eggs, placing the whites in a copper bowl and yolks in large crockery or glass bowl. Add remaining three whole eggs to the yolks along with the granulated sugar. Stir very well with wooden spoon until all sugar is incorporated and the eggs turn a lighter color. Add egg/sugar mixture to the chestnuts and mix thoroughly. Preheat oven to 375 degrees. Using a wire whisk, beat egg whites until stiff. Butter a 12-inch layer cake pan. Gently fold stiff egg whites into chestnut mixture and transfer to prepared pan. Place pan in oven and bake for 50 to 60 minutes. Transfer torte to a rack to cool completely. Sprinkle torte with confectionery sugar and serve sliced like pizza. Serves 8.

CLAIRE GIANNINI HOFFMAN

She is the daughter of A.P. Giannini, who founded the Bank of America. She likes to tell the story of the evening of the great San Francisco earthquake and fire when her father raced to his bank with a farm wagon and two horses, drove through a band of drunken looters, and saved two million dollars in gold and securities by hiding it under heaps of vegetables.

"This is a most appropriate recipe since the area in Italy from which my father's father came was famous for its chestnut trees. This is one of the dishes of the more than one thousand-year tradition of Italy's communities in continuous existence since Roman times. It is important that these still valid traditional recipes do not disappear."

OSSOBUCO ALLA MILANESE
(Braised Veal Shanks)

2 veal shanks (Have butcher cut the veal shanks into six 2½-inch pieces)

¼ cup flour

2 tablespoons olive oil (Bertolli or other fine quality)

2 tablespoons butter

1 medium onion, sliced paper thin

2 cups chicken broth (preferably homemade)

1 to 1½ cups white wine

½ cup finely chopped celery

½ cup finely chopped carrot

1 large ripe tomato, peeled, seeded and chopped

Salt and pepper, lightly to taste

Lightly dredge veal shanks on all sides with the flour and set aside. Heat the oil and butter in a large skillet over medium heat. Add sliced onions and saute until the onion turns transparent, being careful not to brown it. Remove onions and reserve for later use. Brown the veal shanks on all sides in the skillet, adding a little more oil if necessary. When brown, pour off any excess oil. Add wine to the skillet. Cook uncovered about 10 minutes or until liquid is reduced to half. Pour in 1½ cups of chicken broth. (Reserve ½ cup for later.) Liquid should come to top of shanks. Add onions, celery, carrot and tomato and season to taste. Cover, reduce heat to slow simmer and cook for approximately 2 hours turning every 20 minutes or so. When done, shanks should be very tender when pricked with a fork. At this time, sprinkle in Gremolada for the essence of flavor. Continue to cook 10 to 15 minutes. If sauce thickens too much, add some of the reserved broth. Serves 6.

Gremolada

1 teaspoon grated lemon peel

½ teaspoon garlic, very finely chopped

2 tablespoons chopped parsley

LEE IACOCCA

When Congress gave unprecedented loan guarantees to keep Chrysler afloat, it was a vote of confidence in a legend named Lido (after the beach in Venice) Iacocca. Admirers think he knows what this country needs—he already smokes a good cigar, though not a 5 cent variety. Should he run for President, his slogan might well be, "A car in every garage, an Ossobuco in every pot."

GNOCCHI VERDI BURRO E SALVIA

(Green Gnocchi, Butter and Sage)

2 bunches spinach	Grated rind of one lemon
1 cup ricotta cheese	¾ cup flour
1½ cups grated Parmesan cheese	Salt and pepper, to taste
2 eggs	8 tablespoons butter
½ nutmeg, freshly grated	Sage, to taste
2 tablespoons minced parsley	

Rinse the spinach well. Cook with no additional water. Drain well, pressing between hands. With a processor, puree the spinach, then add the ricotta, 1 cup of the Parmesan, the eggs, nutmeg, parsley, lemon rind, flour and salt and pepper. Process for 5 minutes. Flour a large board or counter top and with well-floured hands, form a small amount of the dough at a time into a long roll, about ½ inch in diameter. Cut the rolls into pieces about 1 inch long. With floured hands, roll each piece into a smooth shape. Place the butter and sage into a large shallow bowl. Bring a large pot of salted water to a boil. While the water is heating, put the serving bowl on top of the pot, like a lid, to heat the bowl and soften the butter. Set the serving bowl aside. Gently drop a quarter of the Gnocchi into the boiling water. When they rise to the surface they are done. Remove them with a strainer, drain and very gently put into the serving dish. Stir only enough to coat them with the butter, adding some Parmesan each time. Continue in the same way with the remaining Gnocchi. Serve hot. 6 servings.

MODESTO LANZONE

After a daily swim in San Francisco Bay, he divides his time between his two restaurants, one in Ghirardelli Square, and the newer one in Opera Plaza designed as a showcase for his contemporary art collection. The restaurateur, Genoa-born like his countryman Christopher Columbus, offers a delicious recipe for Green Gnocchi.

THE CELEBRATED CHEESES OF ITALY

Giuliano Bugialli, the celebrated cooking school teacher and author of the award-winning book *Giuliano Bugialli's Foods from Italy* (published by Stewart Tabori & Chang), says: "Italy's hundreds of cheeses, happily becoming better known, are incomparable ingredients for dishes of every course. Many piquant antipasto cheeses go well with aperitifs; a first course may include pasta or risotto prepared with as many as four different cheeses. The grating cheeses like Parmigiano and Pecorino are central to the cuisine. For a main course you might have the classic vegetable pudding *sformato di groviera*. For dessert there are rich cheeses such as the creamy Taleggio and, amazingly, even a sorbet made with Parmigiano."

The distinctive quality of Italian cheese is the result of the ancient tradition of local pride in cheesemaking and a careful nurturing of the beautiful pastures on which the animals graze. The following list is just an overview of the most well known.

Giuliano Bugialli

FRESH, UNRIPENED CHEESES

Ready within days of the milking, these rindless cheeses are moist, soft and creamy in texture. Mild in taste, they are often reminiscent of fresh milk or cream:

Burrata (buhr RAH tah)
  Compact, creamy sweet, shaped like a flask.

Casatella (cah sah TEL LAH)
  Soft, buttery with the fresh taste of cow's milk.

Dolce Sardo (DOHL chay SAR doh)
  White and soft with a creamy, sweet taste.

Fiore Molle (fee OH ray MOHL lay)
  Tinted creamy-yellow from saffron, it is soft, aromatic and slightly salty.

Mascarpone (mahs car POH nay)
  Made from fresh cream, exquisitely delicate in flavor, must be eaten fresh. Sometimes layered with basil, nuts and other cheeses.

Raveggiolo (rah vehg JOE loh)
  Soft, moist, creamy and sweet, from sheep milk.

Ricotta (ree COHT tah)
  Dairy product made from cheesemaking whey.

Robiola (roh bee OH lah)
  Delicate, moist, soft with a perfume vaguely reminiscent of truffles.

Stracchino (strahk KEE noh)
  Made from cow's milk "still warm from the milking." Delicate with a persistent flavor, melts in the mouth.

SEMISOFT TO SEMIHARD CHEESE

Before they are ready to eat, these cheeses undergo a period of "ripening," during which time bacteria or mold causes the cheese to develop texture and flavor. In taste they range from buttery mild to rich and piquant. They may have a natural rind or wax coating.

Asiago (ah see AH goh)
  Made from cow's milk blended together from the morning and evening milkings. Straw yellow colored with many small holes.

Caciotta (cah CHOTE tah)
  Produced from cow, goat or sheep milk or a combination. Generally semisoft and sweet when very young.

Castelmagno (cahs tell MAHN yoh)
  Creamy, green veined, salty and delicate.

Fontina (fon TEE nah)
Delicately sweet, nutty, semifirm with creamy brown rind.

Gorgonzola (gor gon ZOE lah)
Renowned for smooth, moist texture and mild but savory flavor created by soft green mold.

Pannerone (pahn nehr ROH nay)
Resembles Gorgonzola without its mold. Has an almond taste and rosy-yellow crust.

Quartirolo (qwahr tee ROH loh)
An ancient Lombardian specialty.

Taleggio (tah LEHJ jee oh)
Hails from Taleggio, a valley in Lombardy where it has been produced since the tenth century. Flat, rectangular with a tender ivory to orange crust.

GRANA CHEESE
Cooked, pressed and aged, usually for lengthy periods, these cheeses have a grainy, crumbly texture and a pronounced flavor. When young, they make excellent table cheeses; when older, they are perfect for grating.

Montasio (mon TAH see oh)
For table use when young, for grating after a year's aging when it becomes pungent and sharp.

Parmigiano-Reggiano
(par mee JAH noh rehg gee AH noh)
A flagship cheese, production is limited by law to provinces of Parma, Mantova, Reggio Emilia, Modena and Bologna where terrain and forage grant a unique character to cow's milk. Still made according to traditional methods dating back to the eleventh century.

Toscanello (tohs cah NEL loh)
Hard, yellow-white from sheep's milk. Medium sized, delicately flavored.

PASTA FILATA CHEESE
Literally "spun paste" cheeses, they owe their classification to a particular method of production in which the paste, or curdled milk, is bathed in hot whey and spun in long threads until it is transformed into a soft and malleable skein suitable for shaping.

Burrini (buhr REE nee)
Small Caciocavallo type with heart of butter.

Caciocavallo (cah cho cah VAHL loh)
Usually pear-shaped. When young, a mild, sometimes smoky, table cheese; when mature, a sharp grating cheese.

Fior di Latte (fee OR dee LAHT tay)
A mozzarella type fashioned into a braid.

Foggiano (fohg gee AHN noh)
Fatty and piquant.

Mozzarella (moht zah REL lah)
Made from buffalo milk, very white in color, moist and sweet; must be consumed very fresh.

Provola (PROH voh lah)
Spheroid-shaped, smaller than provolone.

Provolone (proh voh LOH neh)
Originally made of buffalo milk, today a cow's milk product. Eaten fresh and young when sweet or aged for grating when it has become "piccante."

Provatura (proh vah TOO rah)
Made from buffalo milk, egg-shaped, small and quite perishable.

Ragusano (rah goo SAH noh)
Compact white or straw-yellow, from the city of Ragusa in Sicily.

Scamorza (Scah MOHRT ZAH)
Shaped like a pear, drier than others of its type.

PECORINO CHEESES
Made from the milk of sheep (pecora), these cheeses are pronounced in flavor and range from soft to hard according to their production methods and age. In addition to sheep cheeses, this category in the broad sense includes goat cheeses as well since both are less abundant than cow milk and more intense. The best known is Pecorino Romano.

Canestrato (cah nes TRAH toh)
Firm and flavorful, name is derived from the baskets in which it ripens, which leave an imprint on the rind.

Caprino (cah PREE noh)
A group made from goat's milk—generally from mountainous sections where goats are prevalent.

Crotonese (croh toh NEH say)
Peppery, strong grainy type blended from sheep and goat milk.

GIANT BREADSTICKS

3 to 3½ cups unsifted flour

1 tablespoon sugar

1 teaspoon salt

2 packages dry yeast

¼ cup oil (olive or salad)

1¼ cup hot water (120-130 degrees)

1 egg white beaten with 1 tablespoon water

Coarse salt, toasted sesame seed or poppy seed
(optional)

Into the large bowl of electric mixer put 1 cup of the flour, the sugar, salt and yeast and stir to blend. Add the oil. Gradually stir in hot water, then beat at medium speed for 2 minutes. Stir in remaining 1½ to 2 cups flour with mixer (if a heavy duty model) or a wooden spoon to make a soft dough. Turn dough out onto a well-floured board and, with well-floured hands, knead it into a smooth ball. Shape dough into an even log or block and using a sharp knife, cut into 20 equal sized pieces for 16-inch sticks (or cut into 16 pieces for 20-inch sticks). Roll each piece of dough into a rope that is 16 or 20 inches long depending on size of pan and oven. Arrange approximately 1 inch apart on oiled baking sheet or on foil covered racks, rolling to grease all side of dough. Set dough in a warm place, cover and allow to rise until puffy—about 15 minutes. With a soft brush paint each stick with egg white and water mixture. Sprinkle lightly with the salt or seeds or leave plain. Bake in pre-heated 300 degree oven for 25-30 minutes, or until lightly browned all over. Serve warm or cool. Store airtight or freeze for longer storage. To recrisp baked sticks, put into a 300 degree oven for about 5 minutes.

TOMMY AND JO LASORDA

A *Playboy* magazine article described him as eager, uproarious, and having extravagant vitality. His "training camp" for becoming a World Series winning manager was the years spent playing for the Brooklyn Dodgers, the Kansas City A's, and the Los Angeles Dodgers. He says his wife and the Dodgers are his two great loves. "Cut my veins and I bleed Dodger-blue."

LYDA LEVI

She is president of the Italian Crafts Council and is herself a fabric designer of note whose crisp patterns can be found in such a renowned hotel as the Cipriani in Venice. In her extensive Milan showrooms in the Palazzo Durini, she showcases the works of Italy's leading artists along with the McGuire furniture she manufactures in Italy and markets throughout the Continent.

QUAGLIE IMBRIACHE
(Quail in Red Wine)

12 quail, cleaned
Brandy
Flour
6 tablespoons butter
2 cups sliced mushrooms
¼ cup butter
1 cup dry red wine
1 stalk celery, quartered
Salt and pepper
Juice of 2 oranges, strained

Rub quail with a cloth soaked in brandy and dust with flour. Melt the 6 tablespoons butter in a heavy skillet. Add quail and sauté 10 minutes. Sauté mushrooms in the ¼ cup of butter, then pour over quail. Add consommé, wine, celery, salt and pepper. Cover and simmer 20 to 30 minutes or until quail is tender. Discard celery, if desired. Stir in orange juice. Heat thoroughly. Serves 6. "Served with wild rice, this is a very elegant but simple to prepare one-course meal. I usually serve it on a platter, arranging the rice in a ring and placing the quails with their sauce in the center. Enjoy it with a Nebbiolo wine, best between three and seven years of ageing."

SPRING SPAGHETTI

3 pounds ripe tomatoes

6 tablespoons butter

12 scallions (including about 2 inches of green tops) sliced

3 to 4 tablespoons fresh basil, coarsely chopped

3 tablespoons fresh parsley, finely chopped (Italian preferred)

Salt and pepper, to taste

1 pound vermicelli

Grated Parmesan

Peel tomatoes, slice them in half crosswise, remove seeds and juice by squeezing, chop and drain in colander. Melt butter over moderate heat. Add scallions and cook until wilted but not brown, tossing them with wooden spoon. Stir in basil and parsley and cook for 30 seconds, then add tomatoes. Raise heat to high and cook sauce for 2 to 3 minutes, stirring constantly, until most but not all tomato juices have evaporated. Add salt and pepper to taste. Serve over *vermicelli*, cooked *al dente*. Sprinkle with Parmesan, to taste. Serves 3 to 4.

GINA LOLLOBRIGIDA

Known fondly to Italians as "La Lollo," she was discovered in true Hollywood style when a movie director stopped the ravishing art student on a Rome sidewalk to offer a screen test. As her international screen career developed, she shared star billing with such romantic leads as Rock Hudson, Yves Montand and Humphrey Bogart. Her hobby moved her to the other side of the camera, and she is now a serious photographer with published books and a documentary to her credit.

RICOTTA PIE

Pastry

1 cup flour

½ cup sugar

Pinch of salt

¼ teaspoon grated lemon rind

½ cup butter (one stick)

1 egg yolk, beaten

Water, as needed

Sift together flour, sugar and salt in a bowl. Add lemon rind. With a pastry blender, work butter into flour until it resembles coarse crumbs. Blend in egg and add water by droplets until pastry can be worked into a ball. Cover with plastic wrap and refrigerate for one hour. Roll out pastry and fit into a 9-inch pie pan. Flute edges.

Filling

1 pound ricotta cheese

1 cup sugar

1 egg

½ teaspoon grated lemon rind

2 egg yolks

2 tablespoons golden raisins

2 tablespoons pine nuts

Diced orange and citron peel (optional)

Confectionery sugar

Beat ricotta with half of the sugar and the whole egg until smooth. Add lemon rind. Add remaining sugar and egg yolks, beating until well blended. Add the raisins and nuts and candied fruit. Pour into prepared pie shell and bake at 350 degrees in pre-heated oven for approximately 30 minutes. If pie is browning too quickly, cover lightly with aluminum foil. Serve cold, dusted with confectionery sugar. Serves 8.

SOPHIA LOREN

The most well known and beautiful Italian face in the world. Her first brush with show business came when she entered a Naples beauty contest wearing a dress made from pink window curtains. Moving to Rome, she played an extra in the film *Quo Vadis*, then rapidly graduated from extra to featured player in a filmed version of *Aida*—with dubbed-in voice provided by Renata Tebaldi. An Academy Award Oscar went to her for her performance in *Two Women*.

"I am happy to send this recipe for Ricotta Pie." Delicious cheesecake from a delicious cheesecake!

STUFFED CALAMARI ALLA SICILIANA

6 large fresh calamari

1 clove garlic, sliced in 3 pieces

2 tablespoons olive oil

2 to 3 cups crushed pear tomatoes

Salt and pepper

Wash calamari under running cold water. Remove eyes and mouth, ink sac and internal quill. Cut off tentacles (which may be added to tomato sauce). Set aside. In a sauce pan combine garlic, olive oil, tomatoes, salt and pepper and simmer for about an hour. If sauce thickens add small amount warm water.

Stuffing

2 cups fresh Italian bread crumbs

1 cup grated Romano cheese

1 tablespoon chopped parsley
(single leaf preferable)

1 tablespoon fresh sweet basil
(or scant teaspoon if dried)

2 or 3 large eggs

Pepper to taste

In a bowl mix bread crumbs, Romano cheese, parsley, basil, eggs and pepper. Mix ingredients until well blended. Fill calamari sac lightly with stuffing about two-thirds full. Close sac with a toothpick or sew. Add to sauce and cook over low fire about 12 minutes. Calamari will toughen if overcooked. Watch carefully. Stuffed calamari cooked this way can be served with rice or spaghetti. Serves 6.

FATHER JOHN LOSCHIAVO

He is the president of the University of San Francisco and the child of immigrants from the Lipari Islands.

"This is my most favorite recipe. It is a dish my mother brought with her when she came to this country. I loved it as a youth and my mother, aged 91 and going strong, still prepares it to entice me home for dinner on Sunday. I assure you it is good. *Pruvartili!*"

MEDITERRANEAN SALAD MARTINELLI

10 tomatoes, ripe but firm

1 teaspoon salt

2 fresh mozzarellas

1 small bottle olives with pimento stuffing

1 tablespoon capers

1 can anchovy filets

1 can tuna

10 cornichons

2 pounds short pasta

½ cup olive oil

1 cup fresh bread crumbs (made from Italian bread, crusts removed)

2 cups olive oil

Salt and pepper, to taste

Dice the tomatoes. Salt and set aside for half an hour. Meanwhile dice the mozzarella. Chop the olives, capers, anchovies, tuna, basil and cornichons. Mix with the cheese and set aside. Cook the pasta 2 minutes less than the package instructs—or so that it is *al dente*. Drain under a quick shower of cold water. Put pasta in a large bowl and add the ½ cup of oil. Stir well and set aside for 2 hours. Put 2 cups cold olive oil in a pan, add garlic and bread crumbs. Over very low heat, cook bread crumbs until browned. Turn off flame, remove garlic and let mixture cool. Drain tomatoes and add to the mozzarella mixture. Stir into pasta. Add the oil/crumb mixture and stir. Salt and pepper to taste. Pile onto platter and decorate with sprigs of additional fresh basil, whole cornichons and olives. Serves 6.

ELSA MARTINELLI

Born in Florence, one of nine children, Ms. Martinelli has made 57 motion pictures. Leading lady to such Hollywood heroes as John Wayne and Burt Lancaster, she was also a world class model and among her multiple talents enjoys fashion designing.

She insists that this unusual pasta salad recipe serves six. This only attests to her reputation as a generous hostess. She is a true lady bountiful for the recipe makes 10 pounds of salad.

SPAGHETTI PUTTANESCA A LA MOFFO

Egg Fettuccini

3 cups flour

4 eggs

Pinch of salt

("I love homemade egg fettuccini, but #8 spaghetti, no egg, is just as good.") Put the flour on a kneading board. Make a medium sized hole in middle of flour and break eggs into it. Add the salt. With a fork, gradually stir eggs, gathering flour from inner circle until all flour is mixed. Then knead dough until it is smooth and firm and begins to blister on the outside. Put under a mixing bowl for about 1 hour. Cut pieces about 2 inches square and roll them very fine. Place them to dry— about 10 minutes. On floured kneading board, take rolled dough and fold up to about 2 inches in diameter. Cut with a very sharp knife into 1/8 inch slices. After each rolled-out piece is cut, open each fettuccini and hang to dry fully.

The Sauce

8 tablespoons butter

3 tablespoons olive oil

4 garlic cloves, finely chopped or put in garlic press

1 can anchovies

20 black olives, pitted and halved

1 tablespoon capers

6 fresh cherry tomatoes or ½ can peeled tomatoes

Combine butter, oil, garlic and anchovies in saucepan over flame. As soon as garlic begins to turn golden (about 30 seconds) add olives, capers, and tomatoes. Stir another 30 seconds over high flame. At the same time, cook pasta in large pot. (See comments.) Pour sauce over it and sprinkle with chopped parsley. Serve immediately. Serves 4.

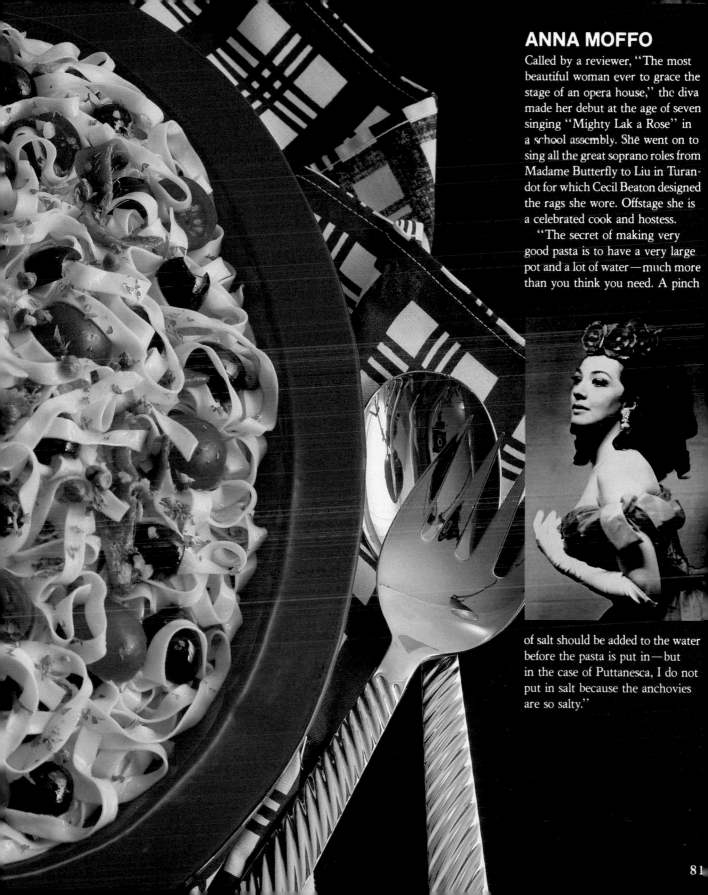

ANNA MOFFO

Called by a reviewer, "The most
beautiful woman ever to grace the
stage of an opera house," the diva
made her debut at the age of seven
singing "Mighty Lak a Rose" in
a school assembly. She went on to
sing all the great soprano roles from
Madame Butterfly to Liu in Turan-
dot for which Cecil Beaton designed
the rags she wore. Offstage she is
a celebrated cook and hostess.

"The secret of making very
good pasta is to have a very large
pot and a lot of water—much more
than you think you need. A pinch
of salt should be added to the water
before the pasta is put in—but
in the case of Puttanesca, I do not
put in salt because the anchovies
are so salty."

NONA'S AGNOLLOTTI

Pasta

3 cups flour

5 eggs

Oil measured in half an egg shell

2 half egg shells water

Sift approximately ⅔ of the flour on to a table making a "mountain." Make a well in the middle of the mountain, and then put the eggs, oil and water in this well. Mix first with a fork, and then by hand and knead. Form a ball, rub with oil, and cover with a bowl. Let the dough rest for about half an hour. While the dough is resting, you should make the stuffing.

Stuffing

1 pound mozzarella cheese, shredded

2 pounds ricotta

1 handful Parmesan cheese, grated

1 package frozen spinach or like amount of fresh spinach

3 eggs

Nutmeg

Salt and pepper to taste

Butter, melted

Fresh sage

Steam the spinach until wilted, drain well and mince well. Combine mozzarella, ricotta, Parmesan, spinach, eggs, nutmeg and salt and pepper in a bowl and mix. (Mixture should be the consistency of thick cottage cheese.) Also remember when adding salt that the cheese is salty, so don't overdo it. Roll out pasta dough, a little at a time, and cut into 3-inch circles. Place a little of the stuffing in the middle of circle, fold in half and seal around the edges. Drop the stuffed pasta pillows into briskly boiling salted water. When they rise to the surface of the water, the Agnollotti is done. Serve with a little melted butter and fresh sage on top. Serves a large family.

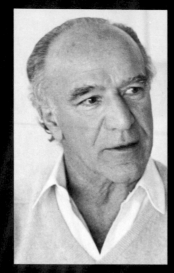

ROBERT MONDAVI

He is one of the major figures in the California wine world and, his operation is housed in a magnificent, mission-style winery in Oakville. The Mondavi family has made wine in the Napa Valley since 1920.

"While we were growing up, the family enjoyed our traditional Italian cuisine—and my mother always used the freshest, best ingredients she could find." Nona, named in the recipe here, is Rosa Mondavi whose directions colorfully call for a "mountain" of flour and the use of halved egg shells for measuring liquids.

CHANCELLOR EDWARD MORTOLA

An extremely well-educated educator, he is the Chancellor of Pace University and holds degrees in philosophy, humane letters, law, and literature. During his tenure, the university's enrollment has increased from 4,000 to 30,000.

"This recipe has been in the family as long back as I can remember. It was my mother's recipe which has been preserved by my sisters. At home we call it 'Zucchini Mortola.'"

ZUCCHINI MORTOLA

3 to 4 zucchini

1 teaspoon salt

3 to 4 eggs

Salt and pepper, to taste

2 tablespoons bread crumbs (Italian style)

1 tablespoon grated Parmesan cheese

Pinch of oregano

2 bay leaves

Peel zucchini. Cut in half and half again. Boil in salted water for about 5 minutes, then drain well. Put on bottom of greased dish. Beat eggs in a bowl. Add milk, salt and pepper, bread crumbs and cheese and stir to blend. Pour over zucchini. (If needed, use another egg.) Put oregano and bay leaves on top. Bake 15 to 20 minutes in pre-heated 350 degree oven. Serves 6.

A CELEBRATED WRITER ON THE COOKS OF CALABRIA

Author of *Honor Thy Father, Thy Neighbor's Wife, The Kingdom and The Power,* and *Fame and Obscurity,* Gay Talese began his writing career fresh out of college when he was hired by *The New York Times* as a copy boy.

"I'm glad you have many flavorsome recipes from the likes of Lee Iacocca and Martin Scorsese and other big eaters for your cookbook. In my case, caring little about food and knowing less— caring only that the restaurants are smart and the Martinis very dry—I've had to write around my ignorance and provide you with the following non-recipe for lithe Italians."

Gay Talese

My ancestors have long dwelled within the vulnerable toe of the Italian boot, an area that for centuries has been stepped on and stubbed by everything from Pyrrhus' rampaging elephants to marauding Magyar horsemen, from Napoleon's charging troops to Hitler's clamorous tankers, from the dusty donkeys of peasant priests to the fleet of Fiats of Mafia chieftains...

and one result of this tradition of chaos and endless invasions of Southern Italian villages has been the evolution of a breed of very angry housewives, who, blaming their wine-drinking bocce-playing husbands for failing to keep the invaders at bay, sought their own revenge by becoming terrible cooks...

The uncommitted cooking done by too many women of Calabria—the region where my people came from— led I believe to the mass immigration of Italian men to America beginning in the 1880's; and, in my particular case, it is the reason why I am unable to list a favorite recipe—for not having learned to eat well, I cannot cook well, and I am uneager to learn now.

Still, my ancestors in Italy and America did have a history of long life— which is perhaps attributable to the fact that inferior home cooking discouraged excessive eating. My grandparents lived to be more than 80; and my great grandparents, lean undernourished aesthetes, lived to be close to 100. Good food to my Calabrian family is very bad for you. We are a proud family of No-Cal Calabrians.

RIGATONI ALLA VODKA

For this particular dish you must prepare two smaller recipes. Purchase a bottle of common vodka and add to it 6 teaspoons of red pepper flakes. Let it stand for at least three weeks to develop full flavor, and then you will use this for the dish. Next, make a fresh tomato sauce as follows: in a saucepan, melt ¼ pound of butter. Put in the contents of 1 can of Italian peeled tomatoes (10 to 12 ounces). Be sure to crush the tomatoes with your fingers so it will take less time to cook. Then add salt and pepper, to taste, and a handful of fresh basil leaves. In 18 to 20 minutes the sauce will be ready. For *Rigatoni Alla Vodka* you will need only 4 tablespoons of sauce—the rest can be frozen for the next occasion. So here we go:

1 pound rigatoni (Italian imported preferred)

6 ounces of the prepared vodka

3 tablespoons butter

6 tablespoons heavy cream

4 tablespoons fresh tomato sauce

4 tablespoons Parmesan cheese, freshly grated

Place the rigatoni into a pot of rapidly boiling water. When *al dente*, or hard on the tooth, drain very dry. On medium heat, place a large sauce pan and put the rigatoni into it. Stir the rigatoni for 2 minutes so that it becomes very dry and hot. Then pour the vodka (be sure to shake the bottle well before using) on the rigatoni. Stir for 1 minute. Put a lighted match to the pasta and a flame will develop. Stir again, and, when the flame subsides, add the butter and the cream. Stir and mix for 2 minutes, then add the fresh tomato sauce. Mix well for another minute, stirring well until everything is smooth, rosy and creamy. Then add the Parmesan cheese, toss a few more times and serve. Buon appetito! Serves 4.

ARMANDO AND ELIO ORSINI

For more than 30 years, the brothers have presided over Orsini's Restaurant, a favorite haunt of the world of high fashion. The fine Orsini taste is evident in the exquisite pink and mauve interior furnished with Italian tile tables and stylish accessories, a beautiful setting for the Beautiful People.

LIZ'S SPAGHETTI SAUCE WITH MEATBALLS

1 link mild Italian sausage, cut into small
  pieces (½ pound)

1 link hot Italian sausage, cut into small
  pieces (½ pound)

2 tablespoons fresh parsley, chopped or
  2 teaspoons dried flakes

1 large yellow onion, cut up (about 2 cups)

4 cloves garlic, cut up

2 large stalks celery, cut up

1 medium carrot, cut up

3 tablespoons corn oil or bacon fat

1 28-ounce can tomato puree

3 8-ounce cans tomato sauce

1 bay leaf

Dash grated fresh nutmeg (if desired)

1 4-ounce can chopped mushrooms,
  drained or sauteed fresh mushrooms

½ to ¾ pound *each* ground beef, pork
  and veal (or combination packaged
  as "meat loaf")

1 teaspoon salt

½ teaspoon pepper

2 eggs

½ cup grated Parmesan/Romano cheese

1½ cups bread crumbs (approximately)

½ cup corn oil

½ cup red wine (Chianti)

1 pound spaghetti or pasta of your choice

Fry sausage slowly in ungreased frying
pan with a small amount of water to absorb
the fat. Meanwhile, put parsley, onion,
garlic, celery and carrot in blender with
¼ cup water and chop fine or use food
processor without the water. Heat the
3 tablespoons of oil (or bacon fat) in a
large pot and saute one-quarter of the
chopped vegetables for 2 to 3 minutes.
Add tomato puree, tomato sauce, 2 cups
water, bay leaf, nutmeg and mushrooms.
Bring to a boil; lower heat and simmer ½
hour. Add rest of chopped vegetables to
the ground meat. Mix in salt, pepper,
eggs, grated cheese and enough bread
crumbs to form unsticky meatballs. Form
into 2-inch meatballs (about 2½ dozen).

Brown meatballs on all sides in the ½ cup
of oil. (Or oven brown; can also use
microwave oven—6 minutes per 12
meatballs.) Add to the simmering tomato
pot. Add cooked sausage. Pour off excess
sausage fat from frying pan, add wine and
scrape all "brownings" in pan over heat.
Pour this into the tomato pot. Season with
small amount of salt and pepper. Allow to
simmer for 1½ to 2 hours with a
"cracked" lid, stirring occasionally.
There will be no "foam;" little oil patches
will form on top which shows that sauce is
done. Makes 2 to 2½ quarts. Cook
spaghetti or pasta of your choice per
package directions. Drain and put cooked
pasta back in the pot in which pasta was
boiled. (Pasta absorbs sauce better this way
and stays warmer for serving.) Mix in
spaghetti sauce. Buon appetito!

JENO PAULUCCI

The story of an Italian packing Chinese foods for the nation in Scandinavian Minnsota is told in Jeno Paulucci's book, *How It Was To Make $100,000,000 In A Hurry.* A one-time hawker at a fruit-stand, he founded Chun King Chinese Food, then sold it for many millions in cash—and gave $2 million in tax-paid gifts to his employees. Moving to another ethnic cuisine, he built a second empire with Jeno's Pizza.

"The very lengthy recipe for Spaghetti Sauce with Meatballs is an absolute favorite concocted by my mother, my sister and myself. Serve it with any pasta such as fettucine, linguine, capellini, spaghettini, spaghetti, ravioli, tortellini, polenta, rigatoni, gnocchi, giant shells or manicotti."

PENNONI AL TONNO ALLA PAVAROTTI

2 tablespoons corn oil

⅓ cup finely chopped onion

3 7-ounce cans imported tuna (Italian or Spanish, in olive oil)

1 2-ounce can anchovies, cut small

3 ounces tomato paste (half a small can)

1 12-ounce can tomato juice

Garlic salt, to taste

1 pound pennoni (or similar pasta)

1½ cups grated Parmesan cheese

Put corn oil and onion in sauce pan; cook until onion is transparent. Add tuna and anchovies and stir for 2 or 3 minutes. Add tomato paste, juice, and garlic salt. Stir well and allow to simmer for 15 minutes. Add to cooked pennoni. Stir well, adding grated cheese. Must be served and eaten immediately. Serves 6.

LUCIANO PAVAROTTI

His musical career began in Modena, Italy, when little Luciano began to serenade the neighbors at age five. He used the apartment courtyard as his stage, its fountain as scenery, and his toy mandolin as accompaniment. And, his audience continued to grow. Not since Caruso has a tenor acquired such an eclectic following. He is also known to be a loving family man, to have brown velvet eyes, and to be an accomplished cook.

HIS EXCELLENCY RINALDO PETRIGNANI, THE AMBASSADOR OF ITALY, AND MRS. PETRIGNANI

A Roman, a lawyer, and a diplomat, he is also an excellent writer who draws inspiration strolling through the gardens of his rolling acres at the edge of Rock Creek Park. Invitations to the Italian Embassy are among the most sought after in Washington because of the Petrignanis' reputation for gorgeous meals served with style and grace.

PENNE AL SALMONE

3 tablespoons unsalted butter

3 ounces smoked salmon (mildly salted)

1 tablespoon finely chopped shallots

Juice of ⅓ large lemon

1 cup heavy cream

2 ounces Scotch whiskey

Salt, to taste

White pepper, a goodly amount

12 ounces *penne* macaroni (dried, not fresh)

Freshly ground black pepper

Put large pot of water on to boil for pasta. Meanwhile, place butter in a large frying pan over low heat. When melted, add salmon and shallots and cook for about 2 minutes. Add lemon juice and mix well. Stir in cream and whiskey. Raise heat just long enough to let alcohol evaporate. Add salt and pepper and stir. Meanwhile, cook pasta very *al dente* (the hot sauce will finish cooking the pasta). Drain well, then gently combine with the salmon sauce until the pasta is well coated. The sauce should be smooth and creamy and should cling to the pasta, but pasta should not "swim" in it. If sauce is too dry, add a little cream. Freshly ground black pepper atop each serving finishes the dish. Serves 6.

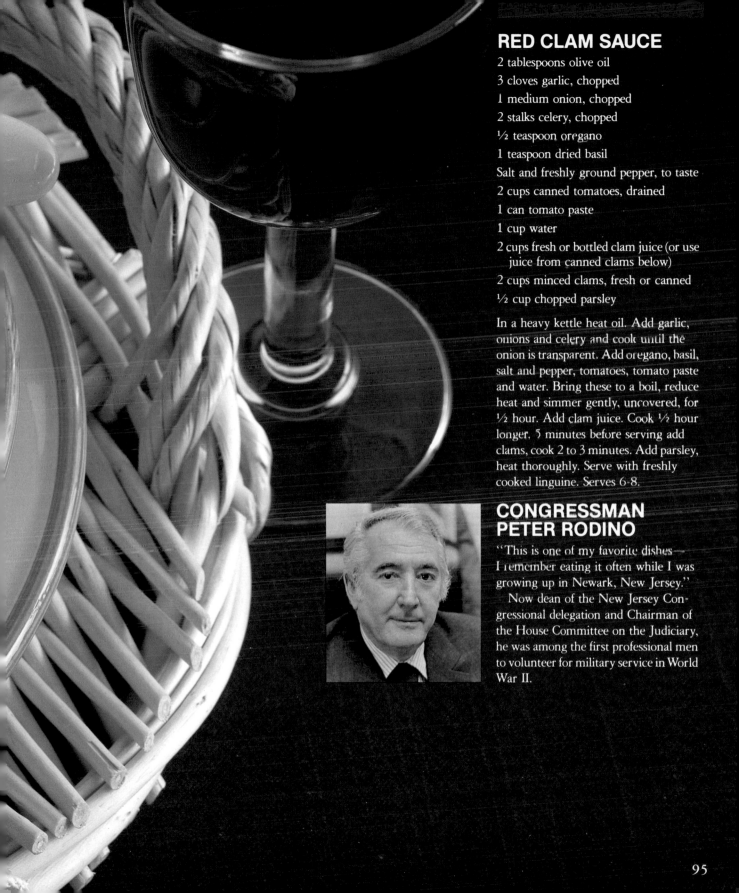

RED CLAM SAUCE

2 tablespoons olive oil

3 cloves garlic, chopped

1 medium onion, chopped

2 stalks celery, chopped

½ teaspoon oregano

1 teaspoon dried basil

Salt and freshly ground pepper, to taste

2 cups canned tomatoes, drained

1 can tomato paste

1 cup water

2 cups fresh or bottled clam juice (or use juice from canned clams below)

2 cups minced clams, fresh or canned

½ cup chopped parsley

In a heavy kettle heat oil. Add garlic, onions and celery and cook until the onion is transparent. Add oregano, basil, salt and pepper, tomatoes, tomato paste and water. Bring these to a boil, reduce heat and simmer gently, uncovered, for ½ hour. Add clam juice. Cook ½ hour longer. 5 minutes before serving add clams, cook 2 to 3 minutes. Add parsley, heat thoroughly. Serve with freshly cooked linguine. Serves 6-8.

CONGRESSMAN PETER RODINO

"This is one of my favorite dishes— I remember eating it often while I was growing up in Newark, New Jersey."

Now dean of the New Jersey Congressional delegation and Chairman of the House Committee on the Judiciary, he was among the first professional men to volunteer for military service in World War II.

MUSSELS ON THE HALF SHELL

2 pounds mussels (about 4 dozen)

1 small jar capers

3 cloves garlic, finely minced

1 teaspoon dried oregano

½ teaspoon dried thyme

½ cup fresh bread crumbs

¼ cup grated Parmesan cheese

Olive oil

Scrub mussels in cold water with a brush to
remove sand. Discard any that are not firmly closed.
Place in a kettle in a half-inch of water. Cover and
steam just until mussels open—about five minutes.
Immediately run cold water over mussels. Discard
empty half shell and any beards still clinging. Place
mussel, centered on half shell on baking sheet. Put
at least one caper on each mussel. Sprinkle the garlic,
oregano and thyme over all. Shake bread crumbs
over mussels. Sprinkle cheese over crumbs. Sprinkle
with enough oil to moisten lightly. Place under hot
broiler for a few minutes until lightly browned,
watching closely that they don't burn. Serve immediately—with napkins. Serves 6.

ISABELLA ROSSELLINI

The daughter of Ingrid Bergman and Roberto
Rossellini, she was raised in Italy and worked
there in both film and tv. A movie critic said of her,
"The camera finds the same sort of beauty, mystery,
and grace in her that it sees in her mother." Today
she is a leading model at the CLICK Agency, and
her face has appeared simultaneously on a dozen
magazine covers.

97

PICKLED BUTTERFISH

6 butterfish, each ¼ pound or more
Flour
1 cup olive oil, or more as needed
1 medium onion, chopped
1 clove garlic, chopped
½ cup vinegar

Clean butterfish and dip each in flour. Gently fry them in a small amount of olive oil until they are golden brown. Remove from the fire and dry them on paper towels. Put the onion and garlic in a frying pan with a little oil and simmer until golden. Keep adding oil until there is nearly a cup in the pan. Add the vinegar and let it all simmer a few minutes. Put the butterfish in a deep serving dish and cover it with the hot oil and vinegar sauce. Allow it to remain in the refrigerator for about 24 hours before serving. Bring to the table cold. This makes a wonderful appetizer, but is also a very good main dish. Serves 6.

ASPARAGUS MILANESE

Cook a bunch of fresh asparagus in salted water until tender. (It usually takes about 15 minutes.) Just before the asparagus has finished cooking, begin to brown some butter in a skillet. Drain the asparagus and place about 6 stalks on each plate. Sprinkle with grated Parmesan cheese, salt and pepper as you wish. When butter is brown and bubbling, pour it over the cheesed asparagus. Some people like a gently fried egg atop this dish.

VINCENT SARDI

Sardi's Restaurant has been the hangout of theatre people ever since Vincent Sardi's parents started it 63 years ago. With its walls of celebrity caricatures and its actors waiting for opening night reviews from the early morning papers, Sardi's means Broadway show business. For carrying on the tradition, he received a special Tony award for "providing the best haven and home for show people."

PASTA PRIMAVERA

1 large onion, finely chopped

2 cloves garlic, minced

4 tablespoons soybean oil margarine, unsalted

1 large can imported Italian plum tomatoes with basil or 4 pounds fresh tomatoes, peeled, seeded and coarsely chopped plus ¼ cup finely shredded fresh basil leaves

4 to 5 cups assorted fresh seasonal vegetables cut into bite-sized chunks. A good assortment might include zucchini, broccoli, carrots, green beans and mushrooms, or substitute your own favorites.

1 pound imported linguine, cooked to the *al dente* stage

In a large skillet, cook the onion and garlic in the margarine until wilted and delicately browned. Add the tomatoes to the skillet and cook, uncovered, for about 20 to 25 minutes until the tomatoes reduce and thicken. Meanwhile, steam the fresh vegetables until they are almost tender. Have a large heated platter ready. Spread half of the tomato sauce on the platter. Top with the cooked linguine. Arrange the steamed vegetables over the pasta. Pour the remaining tomato sauce over the vegetables and serve. Serves 4.

FRANCESCO SCAVULLO

He is known as the photographer of beautiful women. His book *Scavullo on Beauty* is considered a classic. His eye for beauty is evident in his recipe—a veritable cornucopia of garden vegetables. He suggests the meal be accompanied "with a beautiful green salad dressed with vinaigrette. A nice combination would be romaine, endive and watercress. In season, nasturtium, rose, or chrysanthemum petals would provide a lovely and delicious garnish for the salad. Finish this fresh and light dinner with a selection of fresh seasonal fruits." Scavullo also points out, "Not only is this recipe cholesterol-free, it also makes a very good pasta for vegetarians."

THE SAUCE

Singe an onion and a pinch of garlic in oil. Throw in a piece of veal, a piece of beef, some pork sausage and a lamb neck bone. Add a basil leaf. When the meat is brown, take it out and put it on a plate. Put in a can of tomato paste and some water. Pass a can of packed whole tomatoes through a blender and pour it in. Let it boil. Add salt and pepper and a pinch of sugar. Let it cook for a while. Throw the meat back in. Cook for one hour.

THE MEATBALLS

Now make the meatballs. Put a slice of bread, without crust, 2 eggs and a drop of milk into a bowl of ground veal and beef. Add salt, pepper, some cheese and a few spoons of sauce. Mix it with your hands. Roll them up, throw them in. Let it cook for another hour.

MARTIN SCORSESE

The award-winning film director best known for *Taxi Driver, New York, New York* and *Raging Bull* (with actor Robert DeNiro playing Jake LaMotta), Scorsese grew up in Manhattan's Little Italy. He planned to become a priest but went on instead to earn a master's degree in film communication at New York University. The following recipe is the same spaghetti sauce immortalized in his documentary *Italianamerican* in which his mother prepared the sauce. When premiered at the New York Film Festival, the film received a standing ovation and his mother blew kisses to the audience.

INVOLTINI ALLA ROMANA SCOTTO

8 thinly sliced veal cutlets
8 thin slices cooked ham
8 thin slices Swiss cheese
Sage leaves
3 tablespoons flour
4 tablespoons butter
3 tablespoons olive oil
6 ounces dry white wine
1 chicken bouillon cube
1 cup hot water
Salt and pepper, to taste

On each cutlet place 1 slice of ham
and 1 slice of Swiss cheese. Top with
4 leaves of dry sage (1 leaf, if fresh),
roll and fasten with toothpicks.
Roll in flour until completely dusted.
Melt butter and olive oil in cooking
pan. Sauté rolls 5 minutes over high
heat, turning once. Add white wine
and continue to cook and reduce
approximately 5 minutes. Dissolve
bouillon cube in hot water. Pour over
meat, lower heat and allow to cook 20
minutes. Add water to keep moist, if
necessary. Salt and pepper, to taste.
Serve with mashed potatoes or boiled
rice. Serves 4 to 6, depending on size
of cutlets.

RENATA SCOTTO

By the age of four she was performing
—singing for the neighbors from her
apartment balcony in Savona, Italy. As
a teenager she made her debut at La
Scala. Grown-up—at 4'11"—she has
been called "the tiniest package of
high powered soprano in the world."
Her repertoire comprises more than
60 roles, and she is the leading inter-
preter of *bel canto* singing.

As she maintains apartments in
four capital cities of the world, this
favorite recipe of hers carries with it a
special international flavor.

PASTA PRIMAVERA

1 pound zucchini

½ pound broccoli

½ pound fresh green beans

6 shallots, peeled

1 garlic clove

¼ cup chopped fresh Italian parsley

2 tablespoons minced fresh basil

1 pound pasta (a thin spaghetti such as angel's hair)

Salt and pepper

¼ cup freshly grated Parmesan cheese

Fill a large pot with water and start heating it for the pasta. Wash and trim zucchini, but do not peel. Wash and trim broccoli and green beans. Chop all vegetables, still raw, into small pieces. Heat oil in large skillet and add green vegetables. Chop shallots into pan and push garlic through a press into mixture. Cover and steam for 5 minutes. Uncover, stir to mix well and add parsley and basil. Cover again and continue to cook until vegetables are done to your taste; they should still be crunchy. Meanwhile, cook pasta *al dente*. When sauce is ready, season with salt and pepper, to taste. Toss with pasta and sprinkle with cheese. Serves 8.

DANIEL J. TRAVANTI

Born in Kenosha, Wisconsin, he became interested in acting while a student. He attended the Yale School of Drama, did a stint in the army, and then developed a repertoire ranging from Shakespeare to 'soaps.' But he is best known for his award-winning tv portrayal of Frank Furillo, Captain of the Hill Street Blues station house, where he is an advocate of law and order by day and a lady-killer by night.

SPAGHETTI WITH CLAM SAUCE

4 tablespoons sweet butter

½ cup olive oil

2 medium onions, chopped

1 teaspoon sweet basil flakes

1 teaspoon dried oregano

1 large bunch parsley

3 7-ounce cans minced clams and juice

Salt

Pepper, freshly ground

½ cup grated Parmesan cheese

1 pound spaghetti

Grated cheese

Put butter and oil in pan with onions. Cook slowly for about 20 minutes. The onions should be cooked until transparent but not brown. Add the basil and oregano and cook for 5 minutes. Chop the parsley (no stems) until minced and add to the mixture. Cook 10 minutes more. Add clams and the liquid in the cans of clams. Cook for 5 minutes. Add salt and pepper to taste. Add Parmesan cheese little by little. Cook spaghetti *al dente* (about 8 minutes). Pour sauce into cooked spaghetti and mix. Sprinkle with cheese. Serves 4 to 6.

JACK VALENTI

As president of the Motion Picture Association of America, he is the chief spokesman and moral arbiter of the film industry. Grandson of Sicilian immigrants, he was born in Houston, was a teenaged movie usher, a World War II bomber pilot and received a masters of arts degree from Harvard.

"Serve Spaghetti with Clam Sauce, a piping hot loaf of Italian bread, antipasto or mixed green salad and a great bottle of robust Barolo and one can almost hear mandolins and street singers!"

105

RICHARD VALERIANI

As an NBC correspondent for more than two decades, he has reported from all 50 states and 90 foreign countries. He has been White House correspondent, covered the Bay of Pigs invasion, the unravelings of Watergate and, during one three-year period, logged more than half a million miles with Henry Kissinger.

"This is Richard Valeriani live from home and reporting on my favorite Osso Buco recipe."

OSSO BUCO FOR TWO

3 large veal knuckles
Flour
½ pound fresh green beans
2 tablespoons olive oil
2 tablespoons butter
2 cloves garlic
2 tablespoons parsley, finely chopped
1 teaspoon sage
1 teaspoon rosemary
4 lemon peels, finely chopped
1 cup dry white wine
2 cups broth (3 parts chicken, 1 part beef)
Salt and pepper, to taste

Heat butter and oil in Dutch oven over
moderate heat. Coat veal knuckles in flour
seasoned with salt and pepper and brown
in the oil-butter mixture. Mix garlic,
parsley, sage, rosemary, and lemon peel
together, add to pot and cook briskly for
about 30 seconds. Add wine. Cook for
30 seconds. Add broth until it covers veal
knuckles. Bring to a boil, then simmer
until veal is tender. Serve with risotto.
(Marrow of the knuckle should be eaten
with the risotto.) Serves 2.

PASTA FOR A HOT SUMMER DAY

Some summer tomatoes
Olive oil with a strong flavor
Fresh garlic clove
Fresh basil leaves
Spaghetti

Chop and mince fresh, ripe summer tomatoes, draining out most of the water in them to make a paste—but leave some of the tomato bulk intact for texture. The tomatoes are not to be cooked. Add olive oil, finely diced garlic, and chopped basil leaves to taste, and use as sauce for the pasta—cooked not too soft. The sauce is cold, the pasta is hot.

ROBERT VENTURI

Known as the "father of post-modernism," he aspired from boyhood to become an architect. Not only did he become one, he married one—Denise Scott Brown, who is his partner in more than one way. He received the prize in architecture from the National Institute of Arts and Letters "for offering to architecture creative and evocative works in word and material."

"My favorite recipe. It's good for a hot summer day. And good for those with limited cooking experience."

HOT SALAD

Butter
3 large zucchini, thinly sliced
Yellow cheese, grated or thinly sliced
3 large tomatoes, thinly sliced
Parmesan cheese
White cheese, thinly sliced

Place pats of butter in an oblong baking dish or pan. Make lasagna-like layers of zucchini, yellow cheese, tomato, Parmesan and white cheese—and repeat. Put pats of butter on top and set aside until one hour before serving. Bake at 350 degrees for an hour. Serves 4 to 6.

EDWARD VILLELLA

A luminary in the world of ballet, Edward Villella grew up playing sandlot baseball at Queens P.S. 130. Knocked unconscious by a baseball and temporarily out of the line-up, he began to tag along to his sister's dance classes, taught by George Balanchine. A long-standing rule against encores was broken when his performance at the Moscow Bolshoi Theatre brought down the house. An accomplished choreographer and teacher, he gives dance exercise instructions to the U.S. Marines.

"This is a dish you don't have to worry about. You can make it hours in advance and just pop it into the oven an hour before you're ready to eat."

TAGLIATELLE ALLA GRAND HOTEL

Veloute Sauce

6 tablespoons butter

6 tablespoons flour

3 cups fish stock (preferably homemade
  or substitute bottled clam juice)

Salt and pepper, to taste

Melt butter in a large pan over low heat.
Do not brown the butter. Gradually add
flour until totally dissolved in butter. Add
boiling stock all at once. Salt and pepper,
to taste.

12 small fillets of sole

1 pound *tagliatelle* pasta

1 pint heavy cream

6 ounces dry white wine

Butter

Salt

Freshly ground black pepper

Juice from 2 lemons

6 ounces Parmesan cheese, grated

2 tablespoons butter

Put 4 quarts of water in a large pot to
boil and pre-heat oven to 500 degrees.
Meanwhile, rinse and dry the fillets. Coat
the bottom of a shallow baking dish with
butter. Arrange the fillets in it and place
them in the pre-heated oven for 5 minutes.
(As soon as they go into the oven, stir
the pasta into the boiling water.) After 5
minutes, remove from oven and transfer
to an *au gratin* pan. Salt and pepper them
and sprinkle with wine and lemon juice.
Check the pasta—it should be *al dente*.
Drain it and mix with the juices from
the pan the fillets baked in. Arrange the
pasta on the fillets. Cover with Parmesan,
Veloute sauce, butter and cream and place
under broiler to *gratinee* for about
5 minutes. Serves 6.

THE COUNTESS
ANNA MARIA CICOGNA VOLPI

The great lady of *Venezia*, she lives in Dorsoduro, a jewel of a palace with balconies overlooking the canals. She claims, like the celebrity on page 53, that she can't boil water. "To show myself as author of this recipe would cause great hilarity on the part of my friends who well know that I can hardly boil an egg. This dish was created by a master cook of the 30's for the Grand Hotel of Venice." Since Escoffier was the original master chef of that venerable institution, the recipe comes with impeccable credentials.

INDEX